Tin Fish Gourmet

Tin Fish Gourmet

Gourmet Seafood from Cupboard to Table

NEW AND REVISED

Barbara-jo McIntosh

Foreword by Michel Roux

Arsenal Pulp Press Vancouver

ARSENAL PULP PRESS
Suite 202–211 East Georgia St.
Vancouver, BC V6A 1Z6
Canada
arsenalpulp.com

The publisher gratefully acknowledges the
support of the Government of Canada
(through the Canada Book Fund) and the
Government of British Columbia (through
the Book Publishing Tax Credit Program)
for its publishing activities.

Note for our UK readers: measurements
for non-liquids are for volume, not weight.

Design by Gerilee McBride
Interior and cover photographs by Tracey
  Kusiewicz/Foodie Photography
Editing by Susan Safyan

Printed in the Republic of Korea

Library and Archives Canada Cataloguing
in Publication:

McIntosh, Barbara-jo, author
    Tin fish gourmet: great seafood from
cupboard to table / Barbara-jo McIntosh;
foreword by Michel Roux. —New and
revised.

Includes index.
Issued in print and electronic formats.
ISBN 978-1-55152-546-4 (pbk.).
—ISBN 978-1-55152-547-1 (epub)

    1. Cooking (Seafood). 2. Cooking
(Canned foods). 3. Canned seafood.
4. Cookbooks. I. Title.

TX747.M34 2014   641.6'92
C2014-904297-3

C2014-904298-1

CONTENTS

ACKNOWLEDGMENTS

My great appreciation to Brian Lam and Robert Ballantyne at Arsenal Pulp Press for wanting to create a new life for *Tin Fish Gourmet*, originally published by Raincoast Books in 1998. My thanks to editor Susan Safyan, designer Gerilee McBride, photographer Tracy Kusiewicz, and marketing manager Cynara Geissler.

Thanks to Mark Holmes, a fixture in the Books to Cooks shop, for his aid with the recipe development and food styling; to Bethany Leng, our in-shop editor; and to Joan Harvie, who kept the home fires burning in the shop while the rest of us worked on the revision.

Thanks to Alex Waterhouse-Hayward for his patience while photographing me and to John Lekich for believing in me, almost always.

This new edition of *Tin Fish Gourmet* is dedicated to the memory of Veryl, Danny, and my mother.

FOREWORD

I must confess that my friend Barbara-jo's mini-masterpiece, the first edition of *Tin Fish Gourmet*, is my thrifty *frisson*, an indispensable little gem that has rarely left my side. It has inspired many last-minute, tasty meals, when my busy schedule—often spent flying between my different bases—leaves little time to shop, prepare, and cook up anything complicated.

This new edition offers even more endlessly mutable ideas that shine the limelight on the humble and under-rated tin of seafood. The book shows how that seemingly dull tin lurking at the back of your cupboard can be quickly transformed, with the addition of a few fresh ingredients, into an uplifting and mouth-watering dish with minimum effort and maximum taste. One of my staples of choice, the unassuming herring, forms the base of a particularly delicious new recipe, Herring & Beet Lasagna, in which the addition of sweet, pink, earthy beetroot softens the edges of the salty, savory fish to beautiful effect.

This exciting new edition also boasts glamorous photos, which help remind us of the transformative value of simple garnishes that make an ordinary dish brilliant with the addition of something sprinkled, swirled, or trickled, such as herbs, seeds, croutons, cream, or spices. These add that extra dimension—a crunch or flourish to contrast texture, taste, or color—that can make anyone enjoying the meal feel specially treated and looked after.

The most inspirational recipe books resonate with the passion of the author, and here, Barbara-jo's love of food shines through, just as it does in her incomparable shop, Books to Cooks, which is a magnet for the professional and home cook alike. Barbara-jo's new edition of *Tin Fish Gourmet* will be flying off the shelves just as fast as the tins that star in her stunning recipes.

Michel Roux, OBE
March 2014

Introduction to the New Edition

Since the original edition of *Tin Fish Gourmet* was first published in 1998, much has happened in my life. For the past seventeen years, I've been the proprietor of Barbara-Jo's Books to Cooks, a cookbook store in Vancouver, BC, that features a fully working kitchen where visiting authors can showcase their best recipes. I've written two other books, indulged in a love affair with one of my favorite cities by traveling regularly to Paris, and watched with delight as *Tin Fish Gourmet* has sold more than 20,000 copies.

The recipes from the first edition have remained a constant part of my life, both at home and at the shop. More than ever, I find myself coming home after a busy day and utilizing the tin fish in my cupboard. As someone who derives both pleasure and comfort from experimenting with new recipes, I found myself with a growing list of new dishes based on the fundamental concept of adding a gourmet twist to a wide variety of tinned seafood.

The result is this new edition of *Tin Fish Gourmet*, a book of recipes that takes great pride in blending new taste experiences with a lifetime of treasured memories.

Fish has been a part of my life since I was five years old. At the time, my divorced mother began to date a man named Roy who was a commercial fisherman in the summer and a hairdresser in the winter. We began to eat a lot of fish, and we all had great hair. I remember learning how to shuck oysters at the age of six. I remember crying at the sight of all those baby fishes inside the mommy fishes' tummies when we cleaned them, feeling responsible for their deaths because we had cut the mother fishes open. Eventually, I got over it and ate a lot more fish.

This included tin fish, of course. Such classic tin fish dishes as tuna casserole, salmon loaf, and shrimp curry became my childhood versions of comfort food. The tins themselves, stacked in the cupboard to form colorful towers, were an essential part of our kitchen pantry. And, even then, I was well aware of the ease and convenience they provided.

I was also well aware of the process that went into creating tin fish. When my brother turned fourteen, he started to go fishing with Roy in the summer. Tales of the northern regions of British Columbia—the eagles, the ocean, and, of course, very large fish—swam through our dinner-table conversation in great abundance.

Growing up, I was lucky to experience some magical places of my own. Vancouver's Campbell Avenue Fisherman's Wharf was an incredible place. As a young girl, I was overwhelmed by the exotic smells, the sturdy boats, the large totes of fish, and the interesting array of dockside characters. Tearfully, I would watch as my big brother set sail for the summer. I longed to be out on the water, casting my own net.

As the years moved on, my brother left his studies at college to become a full-time fisherman, and I took a job in the fishing industry. Naturally, I fell in love with a man who shared my passion for seafood, so there was always more fish to eat and enjoy. I happily began to experiment with ways of preparing fish. But, no matter how sophisticated my recipes became, I never forgot how to use a can opener.

I even spent some time living in a suite over a fish-canning plant. I found watching the tins of fish moving along the line—with the help of so many like-minded people—to be far more interesting than television. I guess, once you're a fish person, it never really leaves you.

Years later, I tore myself away from the fish business to explore various aspects of the restaurant and hospitality indus-try. After many years of learning from the masters, I went out on my own. But, no matter what I did, thoughts of fish were never very far away. It didn't matter whether I was running my own catering company, organizing unique and splendifer-ous events, or starting my own restaurant.

Appropriately enough, my restaurant's name was Barbara-Jo's. Although fish was not the predominant theme, it was some-how appropriate that the most popular dish turned out to be crab cakes (see p. 53). Other wonderful dishes included baked

salmon with a roasted vegetable salsa, bourbon prawns, oyster and artichoke stew, seared scallops with a lime and ginger sauce, and steamed clams and mussels with a tomato and wine cilantro broth.

But, even as a restaurant owner, I always felt that you shouldn't have to journey far for the privilege of enjoying fish. It's much too wonderful an experience to be limited to those times when your wallet's fat or you simply feel like stepping out to eat. What if you've decided to spend an extra day at the cottage? What if you're simply too tired after a hard day at the office to do much more than open a cupboard? And so *Tin Fish Gourmet* was born.

These economical recipes—tin fish combined with various ingredients that are readily available in any well-stocked cupboard—are updated versions of the recipes I loved as a child. In these lean and mean times, they're designed for those moments when you want to raid the cup-board for a quick, hearty, and healthy—and wonderful—meal.

I hope you find strength, comfort, and enjoyment in the new and expanded edition of this book. It's written for everyone who enjoys good quality tin fish prepared in a simple, tasty, and creative fashion. Much like the key ingredients it celebrates, the original concept has endured beyond my fondest hopes. For this, I look back with affection and thanks to all those who have played a part in my gloriously fishy past.

For Further Reading:

Beeton, Isabella Mary. Mrs. Beeton's Fish Cookery: Including Suitable Sauces, Serving and Carving. London: Ward, Lock & Co. Ltd. [c. 1930].

Lassalle, George. The Fish in My Life. London: MacMillan London Limited, 1989.

Prunier, Simone B. Madame Prunier's Fish Cookery Book. Englewood Cliffs NJ: Julian Messner, Inc., 1939.

McClane, A.J. The Encyclopedia of Fish Cookery. Austin, TX: Holt, Rinehart & Winston, 1977.

The Pantry

THE PANTRY

When I came up with the idea for this book, my plan was to make both the recipes and their ingredients as accessible as possible. For example, I have not included recipes for pastry or special sauces, because they are more time-consuming and difficult to whip up at the last moment. With this approach in mind, here is a list of handy items that, with the addition of tin fish, make up a well-stocked cupboard.

In the Cupboard
artichoke hearts (in water)
baking powder
balsamic vinegar
black olives, pitted
bread crumbs
chickpeas
cornmeal
flour
kidney beans
oil, olive
oil, sesame
oil, vegetable
pesto sauce
pimentos
pine nuts
rice
salsa
sherry (dry)
soy sauce
tomato paste
tomatoes, canned Roma
tomatoes, sun-dried
Worcestershire sauce

In the Refrigerator
butter
carrots
celery
cheese, Cheddar
cheese, cream
cheese, goat
cheese, Parmesan
chives
eggs
garlic
horseradish
lemons
mayonnaise
onions, yellow, red, and
   green
parsley
potatoes
spinach
tomatoes (they really
   shouldn't go in the
   refrigerator, but you
   know what I mean)
wine, dry white

In the Freezer
corn
egg roll wrappers
peas
pastry, phyllo and puff
pizza dough
stock (frozen in small
   batches)

On the Spice Shelf
basil
black peppercorns
cayenne pepper
chili flakes
cumin
curry powder
dill
rosemary
sea salt
tarragon

Anchovies

*T*his misunderstood morsel deserves so much more credit than it gets. Although many gourmets consider the anchovy to be an essential ingredient in a true Caesar salad, some people are a little intimidated by the salty little fish. (Hence cries of "Hold the anchovies!" are often heard when a large group decides to order pizza.) But in countries all over the world, the anchovy is highly respected.

In North America, small herring-like fish such as sprats, pilchards, and alewives are often used in place of true anchovies. The real anchovy, however, is only about 3 in (7 cm) long and is found in abundance in the Mediterranean as well as off the warm shores of California and Peru. Because the anchovy's tender white flesh deteriorates quickly when exposed to air, many people have never actually tasted the fish served fresh. The anchovy must be heavily salted in order to be preserved, and it is often packed in oil. This can create a problem for those on a sodium-restricted diet, those with gout or high blood pressure, or those watching their cholesterol.

But they need not avoid anchovies altogether. A good way to reduce their saltiness and oiliness is by soaking them in white wine or milk prior to using them in a recipe. Anchovies contain niacin and omega-3 monounsaturated fats as well as healthy quantities of iron and vitamin B 12. Used sparingly, anchovies can yield magnificent results.

ANCHOVY BUTTER

I think the nicest thing to have in the freezer is a prepared butter that will accent numerous dishes. This butter is wonderful tossed on pasta or served with grilled steak, chicken, or a strong-flavored fish like salmon or tuna. You just cut ½ in (1 cm) of roll per serving and, voilà! Dinner is served!

Makes about 29 ½-oz (14-g) servings

1 1.75-oz (50-g) tin anchovy fillets
1 lb (500 g) butter, softened
2 shallots, finely chopped
½ cup (125 mL) chopped flat leaf parsley
½ cup (125 mL) pimento, diced

In the bowl of a food processor with a steel blade, place all ingredients. Pulse until ingredients are uniformly distributed throughout the butter.

Lay a 16-in (40-cm) length of waxed paper on a clean work surface. Place all the anchovy butter 1/3 of the way up the paper. Fold the end nearest you up over the butter and roll to form a uniform 2-in (5-cm) cylinder. Tightly wrap ends. Wrap again with plastic wrap and place in freezer.

Anchovy paste spread on bread and butter at teatime was a favorite in Victorian England.

ANCHOVY VINAIGRETTE

This dressing can be used for a variety of salads and can also be used to make anchovy mayonnaise by adding 1 tsp vinaigrette to ½ cup (125 mL) mayonnaise. The leftover anchovies may be used to make Anchovy Butter (p.18).

Makes a scant ½ cup (125 mL)

2 anchovy fillets, chopped

2 tsp capers

2 tbsp lemon juice

½ tsp lemon zest

1 ¾ tsp Dijon mustard

freshly ground black pepper
   (about 2 grinds)

4 tbsp olive oil

In a small bowl, combine all ingredients until mixed well. Set aside to allow flavors to meld.

SAVORY ANCHOVY ÉCLAIRS

I think of the anchovy as the Woody Allen of little fishes—brilliant, but often an uncomfortable feeling surrounds the subject. I love both anchovies and Woody Allen's films, and both deliver strong, complicated, and intellectual morsels worth contemplating with pleasure long after their initial impact.

Makes 13 éclairs

Éclair Batter:

1 1/2 tbsp unsalted butter

3/4 tsp sea salt

1/2 cup (125 mL) all-purpose flour

2 large eggs, cold

1/2 tsp freshly ground black pepper

1/4 cup (60 mL) grated Gruyère cheese

Preheat oven to 400°F (200°C).

In a 2-qt (2-L) saucepan on medium heat, bring 1/2 cup (125 mL) water, butter, and salt to a simmer. Add flour all at once and stir vigorously until mixture masses and detaches itself from sides of pan. Reduce heat to low and cook, beating constantly, for 2–3 minutes, or until batter is very stiff and almost shiny. Remove from heat.

Add eggs, one at a time, beating thoroughly with a wooden spoon to completely incorporate each egg before adding the next. Mixture will initially resist each addition; keep beating until it becomes sticky again and tepid. Beat in pepper and cheese.

Line a baking tray with parchment
paper. Fill a piping bag with éclair batter
and pipe a 2–3-in (5–8-cm) band onto
parchment paper. Alternately, you can use
a tablespoon to mound a rounded shape
(known as a *gougère*).

Bake for about 25 minutes, until firm and
golden brown. Remove from oven and set
aside.

....

Savory Filling:
zest of 1 orange (I use a microplane grater)
3 orange segments, chopped
1/2 cup (125 mL) sliced fennel bulb
1/2 cup (125 mL) mayonnaise
1 1.75-oz (50-g) tin anchovies

In a medium bowl, combine all ingredients
for filling. Keep refrigerated until ready to
use.

Cut each pastry in half widthwise (to
create a top and bottom). Place 1 tsp filling
inside pastry and top with 1/2 anchovy filet.
Top anchovy with 5 leaves of flat parsley,
then cover with top of éclair.

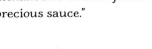

ARTICHOKE DIP  TEMPURA ANCHOVIES

Artichoke dip is great on its own, but I love tempura anchovies, and anchovy and artichoke pair beautifully. Serve this with crackers, bread, or Melba toast. (Best with a dry gin martini, straight up with a lemon twist.)

Makes 2 appetizer servings

Artichoke Dip:

3 artichoke hearts, canned in water, drained

½ cup (125 mL) Lemon-Chive Mayonnaise (p. 58)

¼ cup (60 mL) grated Parmesan cheese

Preheat oven to 500°F (260°C).

In a food processor, process all ingredients until smooth. Alternately, dice artichokes and in a small bowl, combine with mayonnaise and cheese. Divide mixture between two ½-cup (125-mL) ramekins and bake for 5 minutes.

Tempura Anchovies:

1 cup (250 mL) vegetable oil

1 cup prepared tempura batter

6 anchovies

In a frying pan on high, heat oil to 335°F (170°C). Prepare batter according to package directions, Dip each anchovy in batter, then fry in hot oil, 1 at a time, for about 1 minute total. Drain on paper towel. Place 3 anchovies on each ramekin.

The anchovy was consumed in both ancient Greece and Rome. It is mentioned in the works of Aristotle and its unpreserved, fermented viscera were used by Romans in a dressing known as *garum*, "the most precious sauce."

ROSEMARY SCALLOPED POTATOES
with ANCHOVIES and GARLIC

How did this combination of ingredients come about? My mother always judged a cookbook by whether or not it had a recipe for scalloped potatoes. We both loved my cat named Rosemary. And most would consider us both to be strong people, hence the addition of garlic and anchovies.

Makes 2 servings

2 garlic cloves, peeled

3 anchovy fillets

1/2 tsp sea salt

2/3 cup (160 mL) whipping cream

10 drops Tabasco sauce

1/2 tsp crumbled dried rosemary

3–4 Russet potatoes, scrubbed

freshly ground black pepper, to taste

Preheat oven to 375°F (190°C). Place rack in lower third of oven.

Lightly butter a small casserole dish.

Coarsely chop garlic with anchovies and sea salt to produce a pasty mixture. Set aside.

In a small bowl, mix whipping cream, Tabasco, and rosemary, and stir to evenly combine.

Slice potatoes thinly. Line bottom of casserole with 2–3 layers of potatoes. Spread 1 tbsp anchovy mixture over potatoes, then alternate layers of potatoes with anchovy mixture until you have none left.

Pour cream mixture evenly over casserole and add pepper.

Bake covered for 45 minutes, uncover, and bake for 10 more minutes, until potatoes are tender. Allow to rest for about 5 minutes before serving.

FRIED ANCHOVY OLIVES

You could call this a Southern dish or a Spanish dish;
I call it a deliciously global snack. (See photo, p. 26.)

Makes 30 delicious fried green olives

about 30 garlic-stuffed green olives

1 2-oz (55-g) tin anchovies

¼ cup (60 mL) all-purpose flour

1 large egg

1 tsp olive oil

¼ cup (60 mL) fine dried bread crumbs

2 cups (500 mL) peanut oil, for frying

Remove garlic from olives. Halve anchovies. Stuff ½ anchovy into each cavity.

Set up 3 small bowls for breading stuffed olives, containing 1) flour, 2) egg, lightly beaten with olive oil, and 3) bread crumbs.

Dredge each olive in flour, then in egg wash, and finally through bread crumbs, to coat. Place olives on a plate. At this point, they can be refrigerated for up to 1 hour.

In a large heavy pot on medium, heat peanut oil to 350°F (180°C). Carefully drop olives in oil, 1 at a time, and fry, turning occasionally, for about 2–3 minutes, until golden brown. (Be careful when working with hot oil!) Remove from oil with a slotted spoon and transfer to a paper towel to drain.

Left: Anchovy-Stuffed Dates; Right: Fried Anchovy Olives (p. 25)

ANCHOVY-STUFFED DATES

I've been told that they serve something like this at a popular eatery in my community. I love snacks.

Makes 12 morsels

12 juicy dates, with pits
   (to preserve moisture)
1 2-oz (55-g) tin anchovies
6 slices prosciutto

Preheat oven to 400°F (200°C).

Gently remove pits from dates. Halve anchovies and prosciutto. Stuff each date with ½ anchovy and wrap with ½ slice of prosciutto. Place dates on baking sheet and bake for 4 minutes, or until prosciutto is crispy.

SPRING RADISHES *with* ANCHOVIES *and* CRÈME FRAÎCHE

This idea is easy, pretty, and very tasty.

Makes 1–2 servings

1 large radish, sliced into 1/4-in (6-mm)
   thick rounds
about 1 tbsp crème fraîche
about 2 anchovies

Place 1/2 tsp crème fraîche on each radish slice. Top with 1/2 anchovy. Eat "open-faced" or top with another radish round, *et voilà*, a radish teatime treat.

{ Lightly butter radish rounds on 1 side. Dip the buttered side in sea salt and cover with another round. This is a great companion for any tin fish sandwich (try it with Tuna & Tarragon Teatime Sandwiches, p. 154). }

Caviar

Mention the word "caviar" and visions of champagne, black ties, and the Waldorf Astoria come to mind. Caviar seems synonymous with high society, but believe it or not, the real caviar craze only came to the Western world in 1920 when two Russo-Armenian brothers, Melkom and Mougcheg Petrossian, presented the product at the Gastronomic Exhibition at the Grand Palais in Paris. It was received, needless to say, with great enthusiasm.

Real caviar is made from the roe of various species of sturgeon. Interestingly enough, in mid-nineteenth-century North America, a sturgeon wasn't worth more than about ten cents. Nowadays, the roe of the sturgeon is one of the most expensive food products in the world. Here in North America, we can easily get our hands on imitation caviar, which is produced from the eggs of other fish, such as salmon, whitefish, lumpfish, and cod. While not the "real thing," the good news is that these caviars are more affordable and can be just as interesting in texture and taste as sturgeon caviar. And, in even better news, caviar is a tasty indulgence that isn't bad for you! Five hundred grams (a little over 1 lb) of caviar contains only 68 grams of fat and only 1,118 calories (74 calories per oz). And while it may seem a bit salty, 30 grams (1 oz) of caviar contains only about a third of the recommended daily allowance of sodium.

Whitefish, or golden, caviar from Canada's Great Lakes makes up a large part of the processed roe served in North American restaurants and homes. Personally, I like to use salmon or lumpfish caviars in my recipes, but any one of the tasty fish roes available at your neighborhood supermarket will make a memorable and mouthwatering dish. (In Canada, there is Northern Divine, a British Columbia company that produces an excellent sustainable caviar from white sturgeon.)

SCRAMBLED EGGS WITH SALMON CAVIAR

The addition of salmon caviar in this recipe dresses up a breakfast standard. If you are like me, you'll enjoy this dish with a glass of champagne.

Makes 2 servings

6 large eggs
1 tbsp butter
1 tbsp olive oil
1 tbsp chopped chives
2 oz (56 g) salmon caviar
sea salt and freshly ground black pepper,
   to taste
2 tbsp sour cream

In a bowl, whisk together eggs with 2 tbsp water.

In a medium frying pan on medium heat, melt butter and olive oil until bubbly. Add egg mixture and let set for a moment. With a spatula, gently distribute egg mixture in pan. Add chives. Stir again and add 3/4 of caviar. By this time, eggs should be set but not dry.

Transfer to warm serving plates, season with salt and pepper, and dollop with sour cream and remainder of caviar.

It takes 20 years for the female beluga to yield eggs, which partly explains the rarity and high cost of beluga caviar. Due to an alarming drop in sturgeon populations, Russian scientists have perfected a type of caesarean operation that enables them to remove the roe and then throw the fish back into the water alive to begin the reproduction process again.

Left: Scrambled Eggs with Salmon Caviar;
Right: Wild Rice Pancakes with Sour Cream & Caviar (p. 34)

WILD RICE PANCAKES with SOUR CREAM and CAVIAR

The rice gives this recipe a satisfying crunch, quickly followed by the smoothness of caviar rolling over your tongue. (See photo, p. 33.)

Makes 18–24 pancakes

½ cup (125 mL) flour

1 tsp baking power

sea salt, to taste

¾ cup (180 mL) buttermilk

1 egg

2 tbsp vegetable oil, for mixture

¾ cup (180 mL) cooked wild rice

1 tsp chopped fresh thyme

½ tsp lemon zest

1 tbsp vegetable oil, for sautéing

¾ cup (180 mL) sour cream

2 oz (56 g) caviar, for garnish

In a mixing bowl, combine flour, baking powder, and sea salt. In a separate bowl, whisk together buttermilk, egg, and 2 tbsp oil. Stir into dry ingredients and mix until combined well. Fold in wild rice, fresh thyme, and lemon zest.

In a frying pan on medium, heat 1 tbsp oil until bubbly. With a soup spoon, drop mixture into pan to form small pancakes. Cook until bubbles form over surface. Turn and cook until browned on both sides.

Remove to warm plate and place in 200°F (100°C) oven until ready to serve.

Place dollop of sour cream on each pancake and top with caviar.

While early Persians believed that *chav-jar*, "cake of strength," cured hangovers, and Russians claimed that it cured impotence and constipation, today we know that caviar contains 47 vitamins and minerals, as well as acetylcholine, a substance that has been linked to increased alcohol tolerance.

WARM ENDIVE, POTATO AND AVOCADO SALAD WITH CAVIAR DRESSING

*This is quite possibly the most sophisticated salad recipe ever created,
an honor largely due to the addition of caviar in the dressing.
If you don't live in a penthouse overlooking Manhattan,
this dish will make you feel like you do!*

Makes 2 servings

4 or 5 Belgian endives, bottoms trimmed so leaves can be separated easily

2 ripe Roma tomatoes, sliced 1/4-in (1/2-cm) thick

1 avocado, diced

1 russet potato, scrubbed

1/3 cup (80 mL) olive oil

3 shallots or 1/2 white onion, peeled and finely chopped

sea salt and freshly ground black pepper, to taste

2 tbsp white wine vinegar

1–2 tbsp salmon caviar

Place endive leaves in a salad bowl. Add tomato slices and avocado. Toss to combine and set aside.

Pierce potato 3 or 4 times and microwave 3–4 minutes, until just cooked through.

In a small frying pan on medium, heat olive oil. Add chopped shallots and sauté for 2 minutes. Slice cooked potato into 1/4-in (1/2-cm) slices and add to pan. Season with salt and pepper to taste and cook for another 2 minutes.

Remove pan from heat and stir in vinegar and caviar. Shake pan to combine evenly. Pour over prepared salad ingredients and toss to coat well.

"There is more simplicity in the man who eats caviar on impulse than in the man who eats Grape-Nuts on principle."
–G. K. Chesterton

Clams

I first experienced the convenience of cooking with tinned clams while preparing vast quantities of chowder in the high school cafeteria as part of my home economics course. I've always loved the challenge of digging for fresh clams on the beach. And one of the most romantic meals I ever had involved teaming a loaf of French bread and a bottle of white wine with steamed clams and garlic butter.

In North America, there are three primary types of East Coast clams fished for human consumption: soft-shell clams, known as steamers, manninoses, or squirts; hard-shell clams, identified as littlenecks, cherrystones, topneck clams, chowder clams, and ocean quahogs; and surf clams, used mostly in packaged products like chowders, clam sauces, and breaded clam strips. Native to the West Coast are pismo and butter clams, and both littlenecks and manila clams are cultivated in Washington State's Puget Sound area. The geoduck, found mostly in Washington and British Columbia, is the largest clam of the north Pacific. It can weigh up to 11 lb (5 kg) and live up to 150 years. This giant clam is harvested by divers and then canned, smoked, cooked in stews, eaten raw, or fried up in steaks.

That said, making anything with tinned clams is much easier than using the fresh variety. The best news? When you buy good quality tinned clams, you can't beat the flavor.

CREAMY GARLIC AND CLAM CHOWDER

When I was in high school, my home economics course required me to cook clam chowder for the esteemed patrons of the cafeteria. My instructor, Miss Takach, was justly proud of her chowder recipe, and I feel much the same about this adapted version with its accent on garlic. Long condemned as a social gaffe, garlic has undergone a resurgence in popularity as researchers have found it plays a role in preventing cancer and lowering blood pressure and cholesterol.

Makes 2–3 servings

6 garlic cloves, peeled

1 medium white onion, peeled and
   quartered

1 tbsp coarsely chopped celery leaves

1 tbsp olive oil

1 tbsp dry sherry

1 medium carrot, diced

1 stalk celery, diced

1 large russet potato, peeled and cubed

1 5-oz (142-g) tin baby clams, drained,
   reserving the liquid

1 tbsp butter

1 tbsp flour

1 1/2 cups (375 mL) milk

sea salt and freshly ground black pepper,
   to taste

1–2 green onions, sliced

Preheat oven to 350°F (180°C).

In a 10-in (25-cm) casserole dish with a lid, place garlic, onions, celery leaves, oil, and sherry. Toss to combine, cover, and bake for 15–20 minutes. Remove from oven and place on medium heat. Add carrots, celery, potatoes, and reserved clam juice. Bring to a boil, reduce heat, and simmer 10–15 minutes, until potatoes are tender.

Meanwhile, in a small saucepan on medium, melt butter. Stir in flour. Combine well and cook for 1 minute, being careful not to let it brown. Slowly add milk, stirring constantly to prevent lumps. Bring to a boil and cook for about 2 minutes, until it starts to thicken.

Add clams to vegetable mixture, then add milk sauce, and stir to combine. Season with salt and pepper and garnish with green onions.

CLAMS AND STRAW MUSHROOMS OVER LINGUINI

Remember the days when the only thing many families could imagine serving over pasta was meatballs the size of overgrown marbles? Thankfully, things have changed. This fusion dish, an Asian twist on an Italian staple, proves that mixing things up can add a little spice to life. As popular as fresh pasta is these days, I prefer using dry linguini in this recipe.

Makes 2 servings

½ lb (250 g) dry linguini

2 tbsp olive oil

¼ cup (60 mL) finely chopped onions

5 garlic cloves, chopped

2 tbsp chopped flat leaf parsley

½ cup (125 mL) white wine

1 14-oz (298-mL) tin straw mushrooms, drained and cut in half

1 5-oz (142-g) tin baby clams, drained, reserving the liquid

1 tbsp chopped flat leaf parsley, for garnish

Cook the pasta according to the package instructions, drain, and set aside.

In a medium to large frying pan on medium, heat olive oil. Add onions and garlic and sauté for 2–3 minutes, being careful not to brown. Add 2 tbsp parsley and the white wine and reduce for 1 minute. Add straw mushrooms and baby clams. Slowly add reserved clam liquid and continue to cook until slightly reduced and heated through.

Toss clam mixture with cooked linguini and serve. Garnish with parsley.

The word "chowder" probably derives from the French *chaudière*, a large pot into which fishermen threw some of the day's catch in order to make fish stew.

Left: Roasted Tomato & Clam Chowder (p. 42);
Right: Clam & Fontina Pizza

CLAM AND FONTINA PIZZA

The aroma of this dish as it bakes in the oven is a wonderful preamble to how it actually tastes. A favorite recipe for pizza dough adds to the fun, but if you are short on time, try ready-made dough. Either way, this is a unique homemade treat. Wooden pizza peels are available in most kitchen stores.

Makes 2–3 servings

pizza dough for 1 pizza
½ cup (125 mL) tomato sauce
¼ cup (60 mL) pesto sauce
1 5-oz (142-g) tin baby clams, drained
¼ cup (60 mL) toasted pine nuts
1 cup (250 mL) grated Fontina cheese

Preheat oven to 500°F (290°C).

Place pizza stone in oven on middle rack and preheat for ½ hour. Flour pizza peel and spread dough on peel. If using a baking sheet, sprinkle with 1 tbsp cornmeal and place dough on baking sheet.

Spread tomato sauce over dough, then spoon pesto sauce on top. Sprinkle clams, pine nuts, and Fontina cheese over all.

Slide pizza from peel onto hot stone and bake for 8–10 minutes or until edges of crust are nicely browned and cheese evenly melted.

{ While all clams are born and mature as males, some change into females part-way through life, giving a whole new meaning to mid-life crisis! }

ROASTED TOMATO AND CLAM CHOWDER

*Who doesn't like a bowl of clam chowder on a crisp winter day?
This version of a traditional recipe adds roasted tomatoes and pepper with
balsamic vinegar, giving it a more robust touch. You can chop the ingredients
as you like. Personally, I prefer them a little on the chunky side.
(See photo, p. 40.)*

Makes 2–3 servings

6 medium tomatoes, each chopped into
    8 pieces

1 medium red pepper, seeded and roughly
    chopped

2 tbsp chopped fresh basil

1 tbsp olive oil

1 tbsp balsamic vinegar

1 5-oz (142-g) tin baby clams, drained,
    reserving the liquid

1/4 cup (60 mL) dry white wine

1 large potato, cubed

1 medium carrot, diced

sea salt and freshly ground black pepper,
    to taste

Preheat oven to 375°F (190°C).

In a medium bowl, toss tomatoes and peppers with basil, oil, and vinegar. Turn into a medium casserole, cover tightly with a lid or foil, and roast for 30 minutes, until tomatoes and peppers are mushy.

Meanwhile, place clam liquid in a medium saucepan on medium-high heat. Add wine, potatoes, and carrots. Bring to a boil, then reduce heat to medium, and simmer for 10–15 minutes, until potatoes are tender.

Combine cooked potato mixture with roasted tomato mixture. Add clams, warm through, and season to taste with salt and pepper.

CORNBREAD AND CLAM SCALLOP

This recipe was created out of stuff that just happened to be in my refrigerator. Considering that I more or less threw everything together, I was especially pleased at how well it turned out. This dish goes particularly well with steamed spinach and cauliflower.

Makes 2-3 servings

1 5-oz (142-g) tin baby clams, drained
3 green onions, sliced
1 tbsp butter, melted
1/4 cup (60 mL) chopped cilantro
1 cup (250 mL) cornbread crumbs
3/4 cup (180 mL) heavy cream
1/2 cup (125 mL) grated Cheddar cheese
freshly ground black pepper, to taste

Preheat oven to 350°F (180°C).

Butter a medium casserole dish and set aside. In a small bowl, place clams, green onions, melted butter, cilantro, and cornbread crumbs. Toss to combine and place in casserole.

Pour cream over mixture evenly. Top with grated cheese and pepper. Bake for 15-20 minutes, until lightly browned and bubbly.

Crab

$\mathcal{P}$art of the challenge with fresh crab is that you have to earn that wonderful taste by cracking the shell and picking away with tools that take the skill of an experienced locksmith. Your patience is ultimately rewarded, but it can be a very frustrating experience when you taste more shell than crab.

In North America, the most commonly consumed crabs are the Alaskan king, snow, Dungeness, Jonah, stone, blue, and soft-shell. The Alaskan king crab, marked fresh, frozen, or canned, is the largest edible variety in the North Pacific, weighing up to 25 lb (11 kg) and producing at least 6 lb (3 kg) of meat. You can buy fresh, shelled crabmeat at your local fishmonger's for a king's ransom, or you can head down to the supermarket and buy a tin of good quality crabmeat.

As a rule, most crabmeat is canned in its own juices and, due to its natural low fat content, is lower in calories than salmon and tuna. The recipes that I have collected for this section allow you to enjoy the genuine taste of crab without all the fuss.

CRAB RISOTTO

I was taught that it's taboo to mix cheese with shellfish, but risotto is not quite the same without a little Parmesan. Some people think that you have to be over forty to make good risotto because it takes patience. But the time you lavish on this dish is worth it.

Makes 2 servings

1 ½ cups (375 mL) vegetable stock
1 tbsp olive oil
1 small yellow onion, grated
2 garlic cloves, grated
¾ cup (175 mL) arborio rice
1 tsp lemon juice
½ cup (125 mL) dry white wine
1 tsp lemon zest, grated
1 tbsp butter
½ cup (125 mL) grated Parmesan cheese
1 4-oz (113-g) tin crabmeat, drained
freshly ground black pepper, to taste
fresh chives, chopped, for garnish

In a small saucepan on low, heat stock and keep warm.

In a medium saucepan on medium, heat oil. Add onions and garlic and sauté for 2 minutes (do not let them brown). Add rice and stir well, being careful not to let rice stick to pan. Stir in lemon juice and wine and allow rice to absorb liquid. Lower heat to medium-low.

During next 15–20 minutes, add warm broth in ¼-cup (60-mL) measures, stirring well but not constantly. (Do not allow the rice to stick to the pan at all.)

When broth has all been incorporated, rice should be ready. If it's not tender, add more wine or hot water and continue to cook until tender.

Remove from heat, and fold in lemon zest, butter, cheese, and crabmeat. Cover and let sit for 5 minutes. Add pepper to taste and garnish with chives.

CRABMEAT ON TOAST

When I was sixteen, I had a summer job at the Terminal City Club in Vancouver, working in the laundry. It was the toughest physical job that I have ever endured. I did, however, learn two things. One, I never wanted to do laundry ever again and, two, the favorite luncheon dish at the club was Crab Legs on Toast. Although I've never had Crab Legs on Toast at the Terminal City Club, the rave reviews inevitably inspired me to create this recipe.

Makes 1–2 servings

1 4-oz (113-g) tin crabmeat
¼ cup (60 mL) mayonnaise
½ tsp lemon juice
½ celery stalk, chopped
1 tbsp chopped green onions
1 tomato, sliced into 8 very thin slices
2 slices of sourdough bread, toasted
freshly ground black pepper, to taste

In a bowl, mix together crabmeat, mayonnaise, lemon juice, celery, and green onions. Place 4 slices of tomato on each piece of toasted sourdough. Top with crabmeat mixture and pepper, to taste. Place under broiler for 2–3 minutes, until bubbly and warmed through.

Battle of the sexes! During the one-time, forty-eight-hour mating session of the female blue crab, she sheds her shell and is subsequently cradled by her male partner until a new shell is formed. Once this is achieved, the male crab must scurry for his life or be attacked and consumed by his ungrateful mate.

CRAB AND GOAT CHEESE STRUDEL

*Working with phyllo dough is not the easiest thing to do at first,
but after a few times you will feel as if you were born on the Isle of Crete.
You need to work quickly so the sheets do not crumble or crack.
Phyllo dough is available in most large grocery stores and
specialty markets in the freezer section.*

Makes 4 servings

2 tbsp butter

4 ½ tbsp olive oil

7 sheets phyllo dough

1 4-oz (113-g) tin crabmeat

4 oz (125 g) fresh goat cheese, crumbled

¼ cup (60 mL) chopped basil

¼ cup (60 mL) toasted pine nuts

2 tsp dry sherry

freshly ground black pepper, to taste

Preheat oven to 375°F (180°C).

In a small saucepan on medium heat, melt butter and oil together.

Lay one sheet of phyllo dough flat on a clean dry work surface with long edge facing you. Brush phyllo lightly and evenly with butter mixture. Lay a second sheet directly on top of buttered one. Butter this one and repeat process until all phyllo sheets have been layered and buttered.

Lay crabmeat on edge of phyllo about 2 in (5 cm) from bottom edge and about 1 in (2.5 cm) from each side. Cover crabmeat with crumbled goat cheese, basil, and pine nuts. Sprinkle with sherry and ground black pepper.

Fold phyllo dough 2-in (5-cm) over filling
and fold sides over this. Roll up strudel
as tightly as possible. Brush roll with
remainder of butter mixture and place
it seam-side down on ungreased baking
sheet.

Bake for 20–25 minutes, until strudel is
golden brown. Allow to cool slightly before
slicing. Cut with a serrated knife into 6–12
pieces.

The seal of a can was originally tested with a sharp whack of a
wooden mallet. A clear sound indicated a proper seal, a dull one
revealed an improper closure.

KENTUCKY CRAB CRÊPES

This is derived from a traditional dish from the southern United States called Kentucky Hot Browns. I first adapted the recipe for my restaurant, and now I have adapted it for a tin of crab.

Makes 2 servings

1 tbsp butter

1 tbsp flour

¾ cup (175 mL) milk

1 tsp Worcestershire sauce
   (or more, to taste)

½ cup (125 mL) grated Cheddar cheese

2 large crêpes (either your own recipe
   or frozen)

1 4-oz (113-g) tin crabmeat

2 tomatoes, finely chopped

2 green onions, sliced

1 green onion, chopped

1 tbsp grated Parmesan cheese

freshly ground black pepper, to taste

In a small to medium saucepan on medium heat, melt butter. Add flour, stirring to combine for 1 minute. Do not let mixture brown. Slowly stir in milk, stirring constantly, to make a medium to thick white sauce. Add Worcestershire sauce and Cheddar cheese and stir until combined well.

Preheat oven to broil.

Lay crêpes in a low flat dish. Divide crabmeat between them, then top with tomatoes and sliced green onions. Place 2 tbsp sauce on each, then fold crêpes over. Top each with remainder of sauce. Place under broiler for 1–2 minutes, until bubbly and warmed through.

Place crêpes on serving dish and garnish with chopped green onions, Parmesan cheese, and black pepper.

CREAMED CURRIED CRAB AND SHRIMP

Either you like curry or you don't. I grew up on curried shrimp, and there's no question that I like it. Even if you think you don't, try this simple dish. It is so good that it may change your inclinations.

Makes 2 servings

1 ½ tsp butter

1 ½ tsp olive oil

1 small onion, grated

2 garlic cloves, grated

1 tbsp curry powder

1 tsp tomato paste

¼ cup (60 mL) dry white wine

1 cup (250 mL) heavy cream

1 4-oz (113-g) tin crabmeat

1 4-oz (114-g) tin shrimp

3 cups (750 mL) cooked hot rice, basmati
  or plain

1 tbsp each raisins, chopped green onions,
  and plain yogurt, for garnish

In a medium saucepan on medium heat, melt butter and oil. Add onions and sauté for 1–2 minutes, until almost translucent.

Add garlic and curry powder, stirring constantly to prevent burning. Add tomato paste, stir well, and cook for another 30 seconds.

Stir in wine and cook to reduce most of liquid. Add cream and bring to a boil. Reduce heat and simmer until mixture thickens slightly.

Add crabmeat and shrimp, heat through, and serve over hot rice.

Garnish as desired.

Crab talk: A "crab" refers to someone who is ill-tempered; crossing a room "crabwise" means moving in a sideways direction; and "catching a crab" is to miss a stroke while rowing a boat.

CRAB *AND* POLENTA BAKE
WITH SUN-DRIED TOMATOES *AND* PESTO

Some would argue that Italian home cooking is as good as, if not better than, the elegant dishes in the best Italian restaurants. That's because any Italian restaurant dish owes a sizable debt to the kitchens of Mamas all over Italy. This dish is inspired by everything I love about Italian food.

Makes 2–3 servings

½ cup (125 mL) cream

¼ cup (60 mL) pesto sauce

4 pieces sun-dried tomatoes, sliced

2 tbsp toasted pine nuts

2 green onions, sliced

2 4-oz (113-g) tins crabmeat, drained

1 cup (250 mL) yellow cornmeal

1 egg

1 tbsp butter

½ cup grated Parmesan cheese, plus 2 tbsp
   for garnish

Preheat oven to 350°F (180°C). Butter a medium casserole dish.

In a small saucepan on medium heat, stir together cream and pesto. Cook for 2–3 minutes to reduce slightly. Add sun-dried tomatoes, pine nuts, onions, and crabmeat. Add mixture to casserole dish.

In a medium, heavy-bottomed saucepan on high, bring 3 cups (750 mL) water to a boil. Reduce heat to medium-low and slowly add cornmeal, stirring until smooth and thick, about 5 minutes. Remove from heat and add egg, butter, and ½ cup cheese. Mix well and pour onto crab mixture. Sprinkle with remainder of cheese.

Bake for 20–30 minutes, until browned and bubbly.

CRAB CAKES with CAYENNE MAYONNAISE

When I had my restaurant, this was my signature dish.
And like all signature dishes, it has a classic combination of flavors
and textures that contribute to its lasting popularity. People used
to come from miles around for this one.

Makes 2 servings

3 4-oz (113-g) tins crabmeat, drained

2 tbsp tomato paste

1/4 tsp cayenne pepper

1 tsp lemon juice

2 green onions, finely chopped

1 tbsp finely chopped cilantro

1 egg, lightly beaten

2 tbsp grated Parmesan cheese

3 tbsp cornmeal, divided

1 tbsp butter

1 tbsp olive oil

Cayenne Mayonnaise:

1/4 cup (60 mL) mayonnaise

1/2 tsp cayenne pepper

lemon wedges, for garnish

In a bowl, combine crabmeat with next seven ingredients and 1 tbsp cornmeal. Mix until combined well. Form into 4 patties. Dredge patties in remaining 2 tbsp cornmeal.

In a frying pan on medium-high heat, melt butter and olive oil until bubbling. Reduce heat to medium and place patties in pan. Use a spatula to flatten patties a bit. Cook for 3–5 minutes on each side. Crab cakes should be nicely browned and cooked through.

Mix mayonnaise and cayenne pepper and serve on the side with lemon wedges.

SHIITAKE MUSHROOMS STUFFED with CRAB

Sometimes one specific ingredient makes an entire dish. In this case, adjusting the amount of wasabi mustard to your taste raises the recipe well above the ordinary.

Makes 4 appetizer servings

16–18 shiitake mushrooms, about 2 in
   (5 cm), stems removed
1 1/2 tsp butter
3 green onions, finely chopped
2 tbsp mirin
3/4 cup (175 mL) heavy cream
1/4 tsp wasabi mustard, or to taste
1 4-oz (113-g) tin crabmeat, drained
1/2 cup (125 mL) bread crumbs
1/4 cup (60 mL) grated Parmesan cheese
freshly ground black pepper, to taste

Finely chop 2 mushroom caps and set aside.

In a medium saucepan on medium heat, melt butter. Add green onions and chopped mushroom caps and sauté for 1–2 minutes, until softened. Add mirin, reduce for a few seconds, then add heavy cream. Reduce until cream reaches a thick consistency.

Remove from heat and fold in wasabi mustard, crabmeat, and bread crumbs. Taste and add more mustard if desired, and mix to combine well.

Preheat oven to broil.

Divide mixture between mushroom caps, approximately 1 tbsp per cap. Sprinkle Parmesan cheese over mushrooms and season with pepper.

Place under broiler for 3–4 minutes, until browned and bubbly—be careful not to let them burn.

BCLT Sandwich with Lemon-Chive Mayonnaise

You don't have to toast this sandwich, but it's how I prefer it.
Make this recipe for two, using up the whole can of crab.

Makes 2 servings

4 thick slices sourdough bread

2 tsp soft butter

1 4.55-oz (120-g) tin crab, preferably
   Dungeness (better still, leg meat),
   drained

1/4 cup (60 mL) Lemon-Chive
   Mayonnaise (next page)

sea salt and freshly ground black pepper,
   to taste

2 slices fried bacon, drained and cut in two

1 cup (250 mL) shredded iceberg lettuce

4 large leaves arugula

1 medium tomato, sliced into 4–6 slices

Toast bread, butter it, and set aside.

Place crabmeat in a bowl. Add mayonnaise and season with salt and pepper. Combine crabmeat and mayonnaise well.

On each of 2 slices of buttered toast, place 1 piece bacon, 1/2 cup (125 mL) shredded iceberg lettuce, 1 arugula leaf, and 1/2 of crab mixture. Divide sliced tomatoes between 2 slices of bread, top each with an arugula leaf, then cover with slice of buttered sourdough toast.

{ Instead of Lemon-Chive Mayonnaise, you can combine
1/4 cup regular strore bought mayo with 1 tsp lemon zest,
1 tsp lemon juice, and 1 tsp chopped chives. }

Lemon-Chive Mayonnaise:

This versatile mayonnaise can be used with almost all tinned fishes. And you really do feel good after you have made the hand-crafted version. Of course, it needs to be consumed within a few days. I often use a good store-bought mayo and just add the lemon and chives—easy peasy, and very effective.

1 egg yolk
zest of ½ lemon
1 tbsp lemon juice
1 tsp Dijon mustard
sea salt and freshly ground black pepper,
    to taste
¾ cup (180 mL) extra-virgin olive oil
1 tbsp chopped chives

In a medium bowl, whisk egg yolk, lemon zest and juice, mustard, and salt and pepper until smooth. Continue to whisk while gradually adding oil, allowing mixture to thicken. Stir in chopped chives.
Makes ¾ cup (180 mL).

CRAB *AND* SPAGHETTI SQUASH *WITH* LEMON BUTTER

Many people are intimidated by the mere mention of spaghetti squash. It strikes them as hopelessly exotic and, consequently, they don't cook with it. Here's an easy way to enjoy this unfairly neglected vegetable and impress yourself at the same time.

Makes 3–4 servings

1 medium spaghetti squash
2 tbsp butter
2 tbsp olive oil
1 garlic clove, finely chopped
2 tbsp chopped parsley
2 tbsp chopped chives
½ cup (125 mL) dry white wine
zest and juice of 1 lemon
1 4-oz (113-g) tin crabmeat, drained
½ cup (125 mL) cashew pieces or toasted
   pine nuts
sea salt and freshly ground black pepper,
   to taste

Preheat oven to 400°F (200°C).

Cut squash in half lengthwise and scoop out seeds. Place cut side down on baking tray with ½ cup (125 mL) water. Bake for 30 minutes, until strands separate. Remove from oven and let cool. With a fork, separate strands and place in a bowl.

In a medium to large frying pan on medium heat, melt butter and olive oil until bubbly. Add garlic and sauté for 1 minute. Add 3 cups of cooked squash, parsley, and chives. Stir in wine and lemon zest and juice, and cook for 1 minute. Stir in crabmeat and nuts and warm through for 2–3 minutes. Season to taste with salt and pepper.

The giant spider crab of Japan is the largest living crustacean, with legs that often exceed 4 ft (120 cm) and shell width of 1 ft (30 cm) or more.

BUTTERNUT SQUASH AND CRAB SOUP

This soup is quick to make and low in fat, but it doesn't taste like it. The addition of crabmeat adds a special richness, and it is exceptionally nourishing. Rich in fiber, it helps lower cholesterol levels, and includes more than the recommended daily intake of beta-carotene.

Makes 2–3 servings

4 cups (1 L) vegetable stock

1 small butternut squash, peeled and cubed

2 small leeks, chopped

¼ tsp grated nutmeg

sea salt and freshly ground black pepper,
   to taste

1 4-oz (113-g) tin crabmeat, drained

watercress sprigs, for garnish

In a medium to large pot on high heat, bring stock to a boil. Add squash and leeks and return to a boil. Reduce heat and simmer until squash is soft, about 10 minutes.

In a food processor, purée squash mixture (be careful when blending hot ingredients!). Stir in nutmeg and season with salt and pepper. Fold in crabmeat and place in serving bowls. Garnish with watercress sprigs.

In classic Renaissance excess, the banquet presented to Elizabeth of Austria when she made her ceremonial entrance to Paris in 1571 consisted, in part, of 4 large salmon, 10 large turbot, 50 crabs, 18 trout, 17 pike, 3 baskets of large smelts, 3 baskets of oysters, 1 basket of mussels, 400 herrings, 12 lobsters, 50 lbs (23 kg) whale meat, 200 cod tripes, 12 carp, and 1,000 frogs.

CRAB *AND* WATERCRESS TEATIME SANDWICHES

I am fortunate to live in the Dungeness crab region of the world. To my palate, there is nothing better than fresh Dungeness crab. However, tins of crab, when paired with the proper accompaniments, really do shine. Cayenne with parsley, coconut with ginger, and lemongrass with mint are all good partners for this crawly delicacy.

Makes 12 teatime sandwiches

1 4.25-oz (120-g) tin crab

2 tbsp Lemon-Chive Mayonnaise (p. 58)

sea salt and freshly ground black pepper,
   to taste

6 thin slices good quality white bread

1 tbsp butter, for buttering bread (optional)

1 bunch watercress, washed

In a medium bowl, combine crab, mayonnaise, sea salt, and pepper.

Butter 3 slices of bread. Select freshest sprigs of watercress. Divide crab mixture between 3 unbuttered slices and top with plenty of watercress. Assemble sandwiches.

Trim crusts and cut each sandwich into 4 triangles. Eat soon after preparation; they don't keep for more than an hour or so.

Herring AND Mackerel

$\mathcal{I}$ love reading about the history of fish. Somehow, it didn't surprise me to discover that the herring, once a silvery legion that roamed the Atlantic and Pacific oceans in billions, could inspire atrocious behavior (in humans) when its stocks ran low. For example, in 1360, the King of Denmark, seeking to capture the Skane fishery, started a two-year-long war with the Hanseatic League. The first Anglo-Dutch war, in the seventeenth century, may also have started over the herring fishery.

In his 1775 travel narrative, *A Journey to the Western Islands of Scotland*, Samuel Johnson tells us that, "It is held that the return of the Laird to Dunvegan [Castle, on the Isle of Skye], after any considerable absence, produces a plentiful capture of herrings; and that, if any woman crosses the water to the opposite Island, the herrings will desert the coast."

My favorite herring story concerns the Battle of the Herrings, which took place in 1429 near the town of Rouvray, France. The fact that Joan of Arc was involved allows me to believe that I now know the real reason the British wanted to do away with her. Women and herrings have had a long and a complicated relationship!

Kippers are a fat herring, split from head to tail but not separated, then lightly brined and cold-smoked. You can buy kippers fresh, frozen, or in the tin.

Mackerel is actually closer to the tuna than the herring, but I have combined them in this chapter because, when preserved in the tin, they are interchangeable in the recipes. Both types of fish love to be eaten with mustard, horseradish, Parmesan cheese, paprika, or mayonnaise.

I enjoy some of the idiomatic expressions associated with mackerel, such as "a mackerel sky," which is a stormy cloud formation or "as cold as a mackerel," which means to be deathly cold to the touch. In French, a *maquereau* (mackerel) is a man who makes his living from the avails of prostitution, which, in some places, would ensure that he ended up as "dead as a mackerel" if discovered.

MACKEREL PÂTÉ BAGUETTE with CORNICHONS

On my first trip to France in 1983, I scoured the country for the best pâté sandwich. My favorite version came from a food truck in Beaune, parked in the picturesque city square. This is my tin fish version of a beautiful French memory.

Makes 1–2 servings

1 4.5-oz (125-g) tin mackerel, drained

juice of ½ lemon

2.5 oz (75 g) cream cheese

1 tsp creamed horseradish

freshly ground black pepper to taste

1 demi baguette

1 tbsp soft butter

5 cornichons, sliced into fans (make 4
   slices, leave stem whole)

In a medium bowl, combine mackerel, lemon juice, cream cheese, and horseradish. Season to taste with pepper.

Slice baguette in half horizontally. Spread top half with butter and bottom with mackerel mixture. Arrange 5 cornichons in a row on mixture, fanning out slices so each bite results in a full-flavored mouthful. Reassemble baguette and cut in half.

{ Up until 1870, practically all the mackerel consumed in North America was salted. In 1880, the first canned products appeared. }

ROASTED MACKEREL with SPANISH MASH and FRIED LEEKS

On a recent trip to Barcelona, I enjoyed this mash at a tapas bar located in the grandest food market I have ever visited. I was so in love with the market—and with this particular tapas bar—that I ate lunch there on each of the four days I was in the city.

Makes 1–2 servings

Spanish Mash:

2 large carrots, peeled and chopped

1 medium Russet potato, peeled and chopped

1 clove garlic, peeled

2 large leaves Swiss chard, washed and cut into strips

2–3 tbsp Spanish olive oil

sea salt and freshly ground black pepper, to taste

Preheat oven to 200°F (93°C).

Warm a casserole dish in oven.

In a large pot of boiling water, boil carrots for 4 minutes. Add potatoes and garlic, and boil for another 13 minutes. Add Swiss chard and boil for another 3 minutes. When carrots and potatoes are tender and ready to mash, remove pot from heat and drain.

In a food processor, briefly blend cooked vegetables with oil, salt, and pepper (do not over-process; a little texture is both pleasing to the palate and rustic to the eye). Taste for seasoning. Place in warmed casserole dish and cover.

Roasted Mackerel:

1 4.4-oz (125-g) tin mackerel fillets in
    vegetable oil, drained
2 tbsp butter
1/4 tsp smoked paprika
sea salt and freshly ground black pepper,
    to taste

Preheat oven to broil, with rack in middle.

In a small stainless steel (oven-proof) frying
pan on medium heat, melt butter. Stir in
smoked paprika. Place mackerel fillets in
pan, turning until completely coated. Place
in oven and roast until brown and bubbly,
about 3 minutes. Season to taste with salt
and pepper.

Fried Leeks:

1/3 cup (80 mL) thinly sliced leeks
2 tbsp vegetable oil

In a small cast-iron frying pan on medium-
high, heat oil. Add leeks and fry for 2–3
minutes, or until crispy, then drain on
paper towels.

Divide Spanish Mash between two serving
plates. Place roasted mackerels on the
mash, and top with crispy leeks.

HERRING AND BEET LASAGNA

One year, while celebrating Ukrainian Christmas, my dear friend Tadzia Maziar, who is sadly no longer with us, served me her beet borscht with ethereal herring ravioli floating in the magenta liquid. Joan Harvie, who works in the Books to Cooks shop, makes a delicious vegetarian borscht with kale and apple cider vinegar. For this recipe, I have taken ingredients and inspiration from both of these friends to introduce you to a new dish that I hope you will enjoy.

Makes 2 dinner servings

Cheese Sauce:
1 tbsp butter
1 tbsp flour
1 cup (250 mL) whipping cream
1/8 cup grated Parmesan cheese
freshly ground nutmeg, to taste

Preheat oven to 400°F (200°C).

To make the cheese sauce: In a small saucepan on medium heat, melt butter. Add flour and mix well for 1 minute to create a paste. Slowly stir in whipping cream, Parmesan cheese, and nutmeg, whisking continually until mixture is smooth and thick, but pourable. Season to taste and remove from heat, setting aside until ready to assemble lasagna.

Lasagna:

2 homemade lasagna sheets, 4 x 6 in
(10 x 15 cm) each (or dried)

1 3.5-oz (100-g) tin herring

1 tbsp finely chopped red onion

1 medium beet, roasted or boiled, diced to
¼-in (6-mm) cubes

1 cup (250 mL) sliced beet greens
(or shredded baby kale)

2 tsp apple cider vinegar

2 tbsp grated fresh horseradish or 1 tbsp
prepared

½ cup (125 mL) sour cream

½ tsp each sea salt and freshly ground
black pepper

⅛ cup grated Parmesan cheese

If using homemade fresh lasagna noodles, use as is. If using store-bought fresh, cook in a pot of salted boiling water for 30 seconds to soften. If using dried noodles, follow package directions to cook, then transfer to a tea towel to dry.

In a large bowl, mince herring with onions. Add beets and beet greens, cider vinegar, horseradish, and sour cream. Season to taste with salt and pepper.

In a small casserole dish, spread half the cheese sauce. Place 1 lasagna sheet on sauce and spread herring/beet mixture over sheet. Top with second lasagna sheet and pour remainder of cheese sauce over it. Sprinkle with Parmesan cheese. Bake for 25 minutes, until brown and bubbly.

INDO-CAN KEDGEREE

I love this Indo-Anglo dish that celebrates the history and relationship of England and India. I often make kedgeree with a tin of sockeye salmon and the traditional hard-boiled eggs. Here, I use my Canadian palate to create a dish with smoked herring, as I now live in a country that has become intimate with Indian culture and cuisine.

Makes 2 servings

4 tbsp butter

2 shallots, finely diced

½ tsp ground cardamom

2 tsp curry powder

1 ½ cup (375 mL) cooked basmati rice

1 6.7-oz (190-g) tin naturally smoked
  kippers

wedge of lemon

¼ cup (60 mL) chopped curly parsley

1 tbsp butter

½ tsp smoked paprika

2 large eggs

1 tbsp olive oil

½ cup (125 mL) finely sliced fennel

¼ cup (60 mL) flat leaf parsley, stems
  removed

sea salt and freshly ground black pepper,
  to taste

In a medium frying pan on medium-low heat, melt butter until bubbling. Reduce heat to low, add shallots, and sauté for 15 minutes. Add cardamom and curry and cook for another 5 minutes. Add cooked rice and heat through. Add kippers. Squeeze lemon wedge over chopped curly parsley, then stir in gently to mix well.

Meanwhile, in a small frying pan, melt 1 tbsp butter. Add smoked paprika. When bubbling, break eggs, one at a time, into pan. Reduce heat to low, cover, and cook for 3 minutes.

In another small frying pan on medium, heat oil. Sauté fennel and flat-leaf parsley for 1 minute.

On serving plates, arrange fennel and parsley. Top with rice mixture, then with fried egg. Season to taste.

POTTED HERRING (KIPPERS)

*This is best served the day it is made, and is especially good for breakfast.
I like to spread it on a sliced baguette, crackers, or Melba toast.*
(See photo, p. 104.)

Makes ½ cup (125 mL)

¼ cup (60 mL) butter
1 tsp smoked paprika
1 3.5-oz (105-g) tin smoked kippers
sea salt, to taste

In a small saucepan on medium heat, melt butter. Stir in paprika until fat solids in butter rise. Use a tea strainer to remove solids, leaving a beautiful clear butter.

Mince kippers with salt and 1 tsp of clarified butter and place in a ramekin, or any lovely small china, clay, or earthenware dish. Smooth mixture. Pour remainder of clarified butter over mixture to a minimum depth of at least ¼-in (6 mm). Refrigerate for at least 1 hour, until butter has formed a firm cap over fish.

My British heritage encourages my desire to "pot." You can pot all tin fishes successfully, pairing specific species with a spice or herb. (This is where *The Flavor Bible* by Karen Page and Andrew Dornenburg comes in handy.) Try salmon and fennel butter, for example, or shrimp and curry butter.

Oysters
{ AND One Mussel }

You don't have to be a Rockefeller to celebrate the oyster in its many different forms. Of course, oysters in the tin are not for slurping raw with champagne or vodka. But you may be surprised at just how versatile tinned oysters can be. Most of us are aware of how popular smoked oysters are at a cocktail party. And it's hard to resist oysters, either fresh or tinned, when you fry them up with a well-seasoned coating in butter or, for reduced cholesterol, olive oil. Beyond these well-known recipes, tinned oysters are substantial enough to use as a variation in traditional stews and pot pies.

There was a time when oysters were eaten only in those months possessing the letter "r." Oysters harvested in the months of May, June, July, and August were considered unhealthy and even poisonous. This custom was no doubt due to the challenge of keeping oysters cool in warmer weather and the fact that they tend to be thin, watery, and less flavorful in the summer months. Today, oysters can be enjoyed year-round, especially if you harvest them from a tin.

SEARED OYSTERS with SPINACH & BACON

Thanks to the addition of bacon, which stands up to oysters extremely well, this qualifies as one of my favorite recipes. Definitely a sensual pleasure.

Makes 2 servings

¼ lb (124 g) bacon
1 bunch fresh spinach, washed
1 garlic clove, chopped
2 tbsp soy sauce
1 tbsp sesame oil
1 tbsp olive oil
1 5-oz (142-g) tin oysters, drained
2 tbsp toasted sesame seeds
lemon wedges, for garnish

Dice bacon into small pieces. In a small frying pan on medium-high heat, fry until crisp. Pour off fat, except for 1 tbsp. Remove bacon from pan and set aside.

In a pot fitted with a steam basket on high heat, steam spinach until just limp (undercooked), about 3–4 minutes.

Add garlic to reserved bacon fat in frying pan and sauté (do not let it brown) on medium heat. Add spinach, soy sauce, and sesame oil. Cook for 1 minute to combine flavors, remove from pan, and set aside.

Return pan to high heat and add olive oil. When it starts to smoke, add oysters and sear to brown on both sides. Add bacon.

Lift spinach from its juices and place on center of each serving plate. Place seared oysters and bacon on top and drizzle cooking juices over all. Sprinkle with toasted sesame seeds. Serve with lemon wedges on the side.

Pan-Fried Oysters

The first time I had oysters, when I was very young, my mother pan-fried them. I can still taste them now. Then, when I owned a restaurant, we served a dish called Oysters Pan-Fried with Blue Cornmeal and Sun-dried Tomato Salsa. This recipe is a combination of both versions. *(See photo p. 78.)*

Makes 2 servings as a main course

3/4 cup (174 mL) blue cornmeal
1/4 cup (60 mL) grated Parmesan cheese
1 egg
1 tsp milk
cayenne pepper, to taste
2 tbsp butter
2 tbsp olive oil
1 5-oz (142-g) tin oysters, drained
fresh parsley or basil, for garnish
lemon wedges, for garnish
1 heaping tsp flavored mayonnaise per oyster, for garnish

In a medium bowl, combine cornmeal and cheese.

In a small bowl, lightly beat egg, milk, and cayenne pepper together.

In a large frying pan on medium, heat butter and oil until bubbling.

Coat 1 oyster at a time with egg mixture, then dredge in cornmeal mixture. Fry for 30–40 seconds per side.

Place cooked oysters on paper towels to drain, then arrange on serving platter. Garnish with parsley or basil and lemon wedges and serve with your favorite flavored mayonnaise such as garlic, chive, or sun-dried tomato.

Oysters are renowned as a great aphrodisiac. Legend has it that Casanova, the celebrated Italian lover, ate 50 raw oysters every day before breakfast.

Left: Pan-Fried Oysters (p. 77);
Right: Roquefort & Red Pepper Baked Oysters

ROQUEFORT *AND* RED PEPPER BAKED OYSTERS

The neat thing about this recipe is that you can make up the Roquefort mixture ahead of time and keep it in the freezer. This savory butter is good on steaks, chicken, or pork, but unforgettable on oysters. Roquefort cheese matches the power of the oyster, bite for bite.

Makes 4 servings as an appetizer

1 5-oz (142-g) tin oysters, drained

¼ cup (60 mL) chopped red bell peppers

4 oz (125 g) Roquefort cheese

4 oz (125 g) butter

2 garlic cloves

1 tbsp chopped parsley

2 tbsp bread crumbs

freshly ground black pepper, to taste

Divide oysters among 4 small ovenproof dishes such as coquille shells, or a real oyster shell that has been cleaned.

In a food processor, combine red peppers, cheese, butter, and garlic. Spoon mixture onto a piece of wax paper and roll into a cylinder about 2 in (5 cm) wide.

For each dish, cut a ½-in (1-cm) piece of butter and place on each oyster. (The rest of the mixture can be wrapped in plastic wrap and frozen for other uses.)

Combine parsley and bread crumbs and sprinkle over each dish. Grind black pepper over top and place under broiler for 3–5 minutes, until browned and bubbly.

{ It is rumored that Napoleon's military successes were due in part to his habit of dining on oysters before every battle. }

SMOKED OYSTER SPREAD

Smoked oysters on their own are a delight. Many late-night snacks in my home have consisted of opening a tin and devouring the morsels in no time. This more sophisticated recipe can be prepared ahead and served in hollowed-out cherry tomatoes, or it can be frozen then reheated as needed and served hot on bread or crackers, whatever you have on hand. I like to use toasted French bread rounds.

Makes 16 rounds

1 5-oz (142-g) tin smoked oysters, drained

5 oz (142 g) cream cheese

1 1/2 tsp lemon juice

1 tsp light cream

1/2 tsp minced onions

1/2 tsp minced garlic

Worcestershire sauce, to taste

16 French bread rounds

In a food processor, pulse oysters, cream cheese, lemon juice, cream, onions, garlic, and Worcestershire sauce a few times until well-combined but not mushy.

With a teaspoon, place 1-in (2.5-cm) mounds of mixture onto a baking sheet. Place sheet in freezer and freeze until firm (about 30 minutes). Store in airtight containers until ready to use.

When ready to serve this delight, preheat oven to 375°F (180°C). Place mounds on toasted French bread rounds and bake for 10 minutes.

"Shoeing horns," "gloves," and "pullers-on" were a few of the names once attributed to oysters, which were sold in bars to inspire customers to drink more.

CHRISTMAS EVE OYSTERS

Christmas Eve is my favorite day of the season. It is when I like to cook turkey dinner, with a Southern flair, for friends and family. Since I have an abiding passion for this regional cooking, oysters are a very special part of this very special dinner.

Makes 4 servings as an appetizer
or 8 as a taster before dinner

½ cup (125 mL) rosé wine

1 5-oz (142-g) tin oysters, drained,
  reserving liquid

2 shallots, sliced into thin rings

½ cup (125 mL) bread crumbs

1 tsp chopped garlic

¼ tsp ground cumin

1 tbsp chopped parsley

In an oven-proof frying pan on medium to high heat, combine wine and oyster liquid and reduce for about 2–3 minutes. Add shallots and cook for 1 minute. Add oysters and cook for about 1 minute. Remove from heat. (If pan isn't oven-proof, transfer mixture to a shallow casserole dish.) There should be about ¼ cup (60 mL) liquid to cover oysters.

Preheat oven to broil.

In a food processor, combine bread crumbs, garlic, cumin, and parsley. Cover oysters with this mixture and place under broiler for about 1–2 minutes (be careful not to let it burn).

 In ancient Greece, votes were cast by marking one's choice on the inside of an oyster shell.

OYSTER AND ARTICHOKE STEW

This is a rich dish with a sinfully high decadence factor. I used to serve this creation at my restaurant and would lick out the pan after every serving! This stew works well as a main course with multi-grain bread and a green salad.

Makes 2 servings

¼ cup (60 mL) dry white wine

cayenne pepper, to taste

1 ½ cups (275 mL) heavy cream

1 14-oz (398-mL) tin artichokes in water, drained and cut into quarters

1 5-oz (142-g) tin oysters, drained

¼ cup (60 mL) grated Parmesan cheese

2 green onions, sliced

freshly ground black pepper, to taste

In a medium saucepan on medium to high heat, combine wine, cayenne pepper, and cream. Reduce by a third. Add artichokes and oysters. (You may not want to add all the artichokes; this amount is my personal preference.) Warm through for 2–3 minutes to thicken. When mixture is medium-thick, remove from heat and divide between 2 bowls. Top with Parmesan cheese, green onions, and pepper.

 Pearls of any worth are rarely generated by North American oysters, which seem to create only dull, malformed lumps that resemble wads of used chewing gum.

"He was a bold man that first ate an oyster."
—Jonathan Swift

OYSTER POT PIE

I have always found any kind of pot pie to be comforting, but the oysters in this recipe add a distinctly sensual flavor. I have served this with great success using a sweet potato crust, but you may use your favorite savory pastry recipe for tantalizing results.

Makes 2 servings

1 tbsp butter

1 tbsp flour

3/4 cup (175 mL) milk

2 strips bacon, cut into 1/2-in (1-cm) pieces

1 celery stalk, diced

1 medium carrot, diced

1/2 cup (125 mL) oyster mushrooms

1/4 cup (60 mL) dry white wine

1/2 cup (125 mL) sliced green onions
   (both white and green parts)

1 5-oz (142-g) tin oysters, drained

pastry to cover a 6-in (15-cm) soufflé dish

1 egg, beaten with 1/2 tsp water, for egg
   wash

Preheat oven to 350°F (180°C).

In a small saucepan on medium-low heat, melt butter. Stir in flour to make a roux. Slowly add milk and stir to make a white sauce that is not too thick. Remove from heat and set aside.

In a small frying pan on medium heat, fry bacon until cooked but not crispy. Add celery, carrots, and mushrooms and cook for 2 minutes. Add wine, reduce a little, then add onions. Combine this mixture with white sauce.

Place oysters in soufflé dish. Pour sauce over and fold in to just combine.

Roll pastry to 1/8-in (3-mm) thickness. Cover filling with pastry and press to edges of dish to seal. Brush pastry with egg wash, poke with a fork about 6 times, and place soufflé dish on baking sheet. Bake for 30 minutes, until crust is golden brown.

SMOKED MUSSEL <small>AND</small> CHORIZO PAELLA

In the first edition of Tin Fish, *I included a dish called "lazy paella," a tribute to a dear man, Leo Enriquez, who owned a tapas restaurant and made the most delicious paella. He would finish the rice table-side, singing all the while. I miss my Spanish friend very much, and want to share a more sophisticated version of my still-not-Leo-perfect paella, but one that I am, nevertheless, proud to serve.*

Makes 2 servings

1 tbsp olive oil

1 garlic clove, minced

1 shallot, diced

1 tsp smoked paprika

1 whole canned Roma tomato, diced

3/4 (175 mL) cup liquid from can of
   tomatoes

3/4 cup (174 mL) fennel or vegetable stock

1/2 cup (125 mL) Spanish or arborio rice

1 3-oz (85-g) tin smoked mussels, drained
   (reserve oil)

2 whole Roma tomatoes, quartered

1 roasted red bell pepper, sliced to 1-in
   (2.5-cm) strips (I buy these in a jar)

1/3 cup (80 mL) cooked chorizo sausages,
   sliced 1/4-in (6-mm) thick, then quartered

flat leaf parsley, to garnish

freshly ground black pepper, to garnish

In a small cast-iron frying pan on medium, heat olive oil. Add garlic and shallot, and reduce heat to low. Sauté for 2 minutes, stirring constantly. Stir in smoked paprika and diced tomato, and sauté for 1 minute. Stir in liquid from canned tomatoes and fennel stock and simmer for 2 minutes. Increase heat to medium-high, bring to a boil, then add rice. Reduce heat to low, and partially cover with lid to allow steam to escape and cook for 14 minutes.

Meanwhile, in a small stainless frying pan on medium, heat oil from smoked mussels. Add quartered Roma tomatoes and roasted red bell peppers and simmer until rice is cooked. Stir chorizo into rice, then stir in tomato and red pepper mixture.

Divide mussels onto 2 serving plates.
Place rice mixture over mussels.

Note: Do not cook mussels; they are
fragile, and heat from rice will warm them.
Garnish with as much flat leaf parsley and
ground black pepper as your palate desires,
and put on the flamenco music.

Salmon

For me, there are few things more tempting than gently easing a fork into a savory chunk of tinned salmon. A simple gesture, it is filled with mouth-watering expectation, releasing several subtly different flavors at once. Maybe that's why salmon, more than any other fish I can think of, tastes of the sea. And—just like the sea—it's subject to change at a moment's notice. At first it is delicate and then suddenly emphatic as you roll it on your tongue. But no matter how excited you may be to taste it, take a moment to read the label to find out the species and nutritional content of the fish inside.

Chinook, the fattiest and most intense in color of all salmon, boasts the highest content of omega-3 fatty acids. Omega-3, a polyunsaturated fat found in the flesh of fish, has been credited with playing a preventative role in cardiovascular disease and with the lowering of triglycerides. Many studies boast the health-promoting qualities that this desirable fat offers, such as lowering of cholesterol and aiding in the control of inflammatory responses in the body that cause arthritis and psoriasis. The dense and velvety sockeye and the practical pink are the two species you will see most often in your supermarket, with sockeye, the "caviar" of tinned salmon, being the most versatile. These two varieties, although lighter in fat content than chinook, have a richly lingering flavor and are well suited to hot or cold recipes using herbs and vegetables. When cooking with pink salmon, I always add a little more of whatever I am using to enhance the recipe. Pink salmon's leaner nature makes it less succulent and full-bodied than the elegant sockeye, but it's still a wonderful product.

When you open a tin of salmon, you will see that the skin and bones have been processed with the fish. Many people choose to remove these; some processors are even canning their fish boneless and skinless for the convenience of the consumer. I personally love the bones and eat them as a reward for successfully opening the tin. The sensuous crunch is an acquired taste, but the bones can be easily crushed into translucent pieces. Not only is this part of the fish a rich source of calcium, much needed for the prevention of osteoporosis, but its slight crunchiness also adds texture to a recipe.

But quite apart from all of this information, the best aspect of salmon, I think, is that it is the most exciting of all tinned fish.

Susan's Salmon Burgers

Susan is an English friend of mine who, among her many attributes, can boast being a wonderful cook. This is a convenient recipe she developed for her busy family. Not only is it easy to prepare in the manner of a classic burger, but it also has strong appeal for all ages.

Makes 4 servings

2 7.5-oz (213-g) or 1 15-oz (425-g) tins salmon, drained and flaked

1 egg, beaten

½ cup (125 mL) diced onions

½ cup (125 mL) diced green bell peppers

½ cup (125 mL) fresh whole wheat bread crumbs

1 tbsp lemon juice

1 tsp grated lemon peel, or more, to taste

½ tsp crushed dried rosemary

freshly ground black pepper, to taste

1 tbsp vegetable oil

Combine all ingredients except oil and mix to combine well. Form into 4 or 5 patties.

In a frying pan on medium, heat oil. Cook patties about 3–4 minutes per side, until lightly browned on each side. Serve on toasted hamburger buns with your favorite toppings (lettuce, tomato, etc.).

The first mechanization of salmon canning occurred in 1906 with a daunting-looking machine that beheaded, gutted, and washed the fish in rapid succession.

SALMON *AND* FENNEL STEW

When I worked for fabled Vancouver restaurateur Umberto Menghi many moons ago, we used to serve a unique entrée with fresh salmon and fennel. This is a different recipe that has all the comforting qualities of a faithful stew but retains the same tempting combination of flavors.

Makes 2–3 servings

1 tbsp butter

1 ½ tsp olive oil

1 garlic clove, sliced

1 small fennel bulb, sliced (reserve fronds for garnish)

1 small red bell pepper, chopped

4 small tomatoes, quartered

2 green onions, sliced

30 spinach leaves

1 7.5-oz (213-g) tin salmon, drained

freshly ground black pepper, to taste

In a medium saucepan on medium heat, melt butter and oil. Add garlic and fennel and sauté for about 30 seconds. Stir in red pepper and tomatoes. Cover pan, reduce heat to low, and simmer for 10 minutes. When mixture is soft and flavorful, remove from heat and add green onions, spinach, and chunks of salmon. Return pan to medium heat and cook to warm through, about 1–2 minutes. Season with pepper.

Garnish with fennel fronds.

SALMON  CHEDDAR QUICHE

This dish is based on one of the first recipes that I, as a beginner cook, ever made with tinned salmon. At the time, I thought it was a terribly sophisticated way to entertain. Whenever I make this now, I remember cooking it for my girlfriends and feeling very "continental."

Makes 4 servings

1 9-in (23-cm) pastry shell
1 7.5-oz (213-g) tin salmon, drained and
  flaked
1 cup (250 mL) grated Cheddar cheese
1/4 cup (60 mL) sliced green onions
5 fresh basil leaves, sliced (or 1/2 tsp dried)
2 tbsp chopped pimento
2 large eggs
1 cup (125 mL) light cream
freshly ground black pepper, to taste
1/4 cup (60 mL) grated Parmesan cheese

Preheat oven to 375°F (190°C). Place rack in middle of oven.

Bake pastry shell for 10 minutes. Remove shell from oven and lower heat to 350°F (180°C).

Distribute salmon evenly over pastry shell. Cover with Cheddar cheese, onions, basil, and pimento.

Beat eggs well with cream and pepper. Pour over salmon mixture and sprinkle with Parmesan cheese. Bake for 30 minutes.

Allow to sit for a moment before you slice and serve.

 While Pacific salmon die after spawning once, some Atlantic salmon are able to spawn several times in a lifetime.

CURRIED SALMON LOAF

I grew up with a basic salmon loaf that my granny called her own. She was an English cook, and it was a staple of her recipe files. It continues to remind me of her and I love the memory, but I had to create my own version to satisfy my spicier palate.

Makes 2 servings

1 tsp butter

1 tbsp butter

1 ½ tsp curry powder

1 large green onion, sliced

1 medium tomato, finely chopped

1 small carrot, grated

1 small parsnip, grated

1 7.5-oz (213-g) tin salmon, drained

1 egg

¼ cup (60 mL) grated Parmesan cheese

2 lemon wedges, for garnish

Preheat oven to 350°F (180°C). Place rack in middle of oven.

Butter an 8-in (20-cm) loaf pan with 1 tsp butter and set aside.

In a small saucepan on medium heat, melt 1 tbsp butter. Stir in curry powder and cook for 30 seconds, being careful not to let it burn. Stir in green onions, tomatoes, carrots, and parsnip and reduce heat to medium-low. Cover saucepan and cook for 2 minutes.

Remove from heat and turn into a bowl. Add salmon, egg, and Parmesan cheese. Mix until just combined but not mushy. Place in loaf pan, cover with parchment paper, and bake for 35 minutes. Remove cover and cook for 2 more minutes.

Serve loaf slices with lemon wedges.

SWISS CHARD AND SALMON LASAGNA

This recipe is somewhat fussy, but it will be sure to impress your most discriminating guests. To add a more dramatic flair, use the heartier shiitake mushroom. For increased richness that is impossible for the true gourmet to resist, you can use heavy cream instead of milk for the béchamel sauce.

Makes 4 servings

Béchamel Sauce:

1 tbsp butter

1 tbsp flour

1 1/3 cups (325 mL) milk

Lasagna:

6 large Swiss chard leaves

1 1/2 cups (375 mL) ricotta cheese

1/3 cup (75 mL) grated Parmesan cheese

1 egg

1 tbsp olive oil

2 garlic cloves, sliced

1/2 lb (250 g) sliced mushrooms

2 green onions, sliced

1 7.5-oz (213-g) tin salmon, drained

5 tbsp grated Parmesan cheese

In a small saucepan on medium-low heat, melt butter. Stir in flour with a wooden spoon for 1 minute, being careful not to let it burn. Add milk slowly, stirring constantly until sauce is thick. Remove from heat and set aside.

Preheat oven to 350°F (180°C). Place rack in middle of oven.

In a pot fitted with a steamer on high heat, steam chard leaves for 30 seconds. Remove from heat and set aside.

In a bowl, combine ricotta cheese, 1/3 cup (75 mL) Parmesan cheese, and egg, and set aside.

In a frying pan on medium, heat oil. Add garlic, mushrooms, and green onions and sauté gently for 3–5 minutes, until mushrooms are limp.

Line bottom of an 11-in (28-cm) casserole dish with 1/3 of béchamel sauce. Top with 2 chard leaves. Place 1/2 of mushroom mixture on chard and 1/2 tin of salmon over mushrooms. Pour 1/2 ricotta mixture over salmon and cover with 2 more chard leaves, remainder of mushroom mixture, salmon, ricotta, and last 2 chard leaves. Cover entire mixture with remainder of béchamel and sprinkle with remainder of Parmesan cheese.

Bake for 40 minutes. Remove from oven and let sit for a moment before slicing into portions.

CORN ⁓ SALMON FRITTERS

This is a traditional Southern recipe that becomes a substantial appetizer with the addition of salmon. Add a salad and you've got a delicious meal. Be careful not to overcook it or you'll lose the wonderful melt-in-your-mouth sensation that makes this dish so terrific.

Makes 2–3 servings

1 ½ tsp sugar

1 tsp baking powder

½ tsp baking soda

1 cup (250 mL) all-purpose flour

¾ cup (175 mL) milk

2 tbsp butter, melted

2 eggs

2 tbsp diced red bell pepper

2 tbsp diced celery

1 green onion, sliced

¼ cup (60 mL) kernel corn (fresh if in season, or frozen)

1 3.75-oz (106-g) tin salmon, drained

¼ cup (60 mL) grated cheddar cheese

vegetable oil, for frying

In a large bowl, combine sugar, baking powder, baking soda, and flour.

In a separate bowl, combine milk, butter, and eggs. In a thin and steady stream, add milk mixture to dry ingredients and gently fold batter with rubber spatula. Do not over mix. Fold in red bell pepper, celery, onions, corn, salmon, and cheese (the batter will be lumpy).

In a large frying pan on medium-high, heat ½-in (1 cm) oil until a small bit of batter dropped into oil bubbles (about 375°F/190°C). With a ¼-cup (60-mL) measure filled about ¾ full, drop batter into oil. Fry 2 minutes per side, until golden brown. Drain on paper towels for about 2 minutes.

Salmon will swim, without feeding, up to 3,000 miles (4,800 km) to spawn. Some believe that salmon can return to the exact spot where they hatched using their sense of smell.

SALMON <small>AND</small> POTATO SALAD

Potato salad comes in many appetizing variations, and I love them all. And, with the welcome addition of salmon, it becomes my "desert island dish." A restaurant in my neighborhood gave me the inspiration for this spicy recipe.

Makes 2–3 servings

½ cup (125 mL) sour cream

1 tbsp creamed horseradish

1 bunch watercress, torn into sections

½ lb (250 g) nugget potatoes, cooked and cooled

3 green onions, sliced

1 celery stalk, diced

1 7.5-oz (213-g) tin salmon, drained

freshly ground black pepper, to taste

In a small bowl, combine sour cream and horseradish and set aside. Line a shallow salad bowl with watercress.

Cut potatoes in half and place in a separate bowl. Add onions, celery, and salmon. Toss with sour cream mixture, then transfer to salad bowl. Season with pepper and top with a sprig of watercress.

{ Freshness that lasts! According to legend, canned BC salmon that was shipped off to allied troops in World War I was hidden and then discovered and eaten by a new generation of troops during World War II. }

AVOCADO, CHICKPEA and SALMON SALAD

This summer salad proves that salmon does well on the cool side. It gives you a quick but elegant way to entertain on a steamy August night after a full day's work. All three main ingredients are rich sources of protein, making this recipe a winner for those following a high-protein diet. And don't shy away from avocados because you think they're high in fat—it's monounsaturated fat, not the cholesterol-raising type.

Makes 2–4 servings

Dressing:

1 tbsp curry powder

2 tbsp apple cider vinegar

¼ cup (60 mL) olive oil

Salad:

3 leaves butter lettuce

6 spinach leaves

1 7.5-oz (213-g) tin salmon, drained

1 cup (250 mL) canned chickpeas, drained

3 green onions, sliced

2 radishes, cut into thin wedges

¼ cup (60 mL) grated carrots

¼ cup (60 mL) grated zucchini

1 avocado, sliced into wedges

1 ripe tomato, sliced into wedges

In a small bowl, combine dressing ingredients and set aside.

In a 10-in (25-cm) shallow bowl, arrange lettuce and spinach leaves. Add salmon, chickpeas, onions, radishes, carrots, and zucchini. Arrange avocado and tomato wedges alternately around perimeter of bowl.

Just before serving, give dressing a stir, pour over salad, and toss to combine.

SALMON AND BROCCOLI CHOWDER

I created this dish out of necessity as comfort food on a rainy November evening. It is a thick chowder that could almost be classified as a stew—but soup has its own special magic. A few contemplative spoonfuls of this on a cold night may conjure up welcome memories of your mother's classic creations.

Makes 2–3 servings

1 tbsp butter

1 small red onion, sliced into rings then cut in half

1 tbsp flour

1 tsp chopped fresh thyme or 1/2 tsp dried

2 cups (500 mL) hot milk

1 7.5-oz (213-g) tin salmon, drained and flaked

1 cup (250 mL) cooked and diced potatoes

1 cup (250 mL) steamed broccoli florets

1/4 cup (60 mL) grated Parmesan cheese

1 tbsp chopped fresh chives, for garnish

freshly ground black pepper, to taste

In a large saucepan on medium-high heat, melt butter until foam subsides. Reduce heat to medium. Add onions and sauté for 2 minutes, but don't let them brown.

Stir in flour until onions are coated. Add thyme.

Slowly add milk, stirring constantly, until mixture is thick and creamy. Add salmon, potatoes, and broccoli and heat through. Serve in bowls and sprinkle with Parmesan cheese, chives, and pepper.

ASPARAGUS, BRIE ∞ SALMON OMELETTE

My wandering friends are always returning home with tales of fabulous meals that they have experienced on their travels. This particular idea came from a friend who extolled the many virtues of a lunch he had enjoyed on a recent visit to Manhattan. He was so enthusiastic that I created my own version.

Makes 2 servings

1 tbsp butter

4 eggs, lightly beaten with 1 tbsp water

1 3.25-oz (106-g) tin salmon, drained

3 oz Brie cheese, sliced thinly

8 asparagus stalks, trimmed and steamed
   for 3–4 minutes

In a 10-in (25-cm) frying pan on medium-high heat, melt butter. When foam subsides, reduce heat to medium-low.

Pour eggs into pan and let sit undisturbed for 15 seconds. With rubber spatula, gently move mixture around pan. Flake salmon over eggs, leaving a 1-in (2.5-cm) border around perimeter of omelette. Add cheese and asparagus.

With a spatula, fold omelette in half. Then, either flip it over or cover pan with a lid for 1–2 minutes, just long enough to set but still be creamy inside.

 Pacific salmon occur in an estimated 1,300 to 1,500 rivers and streams in British Columbia and have been successfully introduced into New Zealand, parts of Eurasia, the Great Lakes, and South America. Today, approximately sixty percent of the world's salmon is farmed. Most farmed salmon comes from Norway, Chile, Scotland, and Canada.

MUSHROOM, SALMON and SPINACH FRITTATA

Sometimes, you never know what you'll come up with until you begin to experiment with leftovers in the refrigerator. I developed this recipe one leisurely Sunday morning and was surprised to discover how well the improvised marriage of ingredients worked. Now it's a regular part of my weekend whenever I'm entertaining for brunch.

Makes 2–3 servings

4 eggs, lightly beaten

¼ cup (60 mL) milk

1 cup (250 mL) cooked and sliced potatoes

1 firmly packed cup (250 mL) steamed
   spinach

1 cup (250 mL) sautéed mushrooms

2 green onions, sliced

1 7.5-oz (213-g) tin salmon, drained

1 cup grated cheddar cheese

sea salt and freshly ground black pepper,
   to taste

Preheat oven to 400°F (200°C). Lightly oil a casserole dish.

In a bowl, beat together eggs and milk.

In a casserole dish, layer remaining ingredients in order listed. Sprinkle a dash of salt and pepper between each layer. Cover all with egg mixture.

Bake for 20–30 minutes.

NEW ENGLAND SALMON CAKES

A traditional New England salmon dinner consists of salmon, peas, and boiled potatoes, which often end up mashed together on the plate in a comforting swirl. This is a recipe in which my two favorite things come together: salmon cakes and New England. It's a great dish to prepare from leftovers. Served with dill mayonnaise and lemon wedges, it turns into something that seems brand new!

Makes 2 servings

1 7.5-oz (213-g) tin salmon, drained

1 cup (250 mL) mashed potatoes

½ cup (125 mL) cooked fresh or frozen peas

1 egg, lightly beaten

1 green onion, sliced

1 ½ tsp fresh dill or ½ tsp dried

sea salt and freshly ground black pepper, to taste

2 tbsp whole wheat flour

1 tbsp butter

1 tbsp vegetable oil

In a large bowl, combine all ingredients except flour, butter, and oil. Form mixture into 4 patties and dredge in flour.

In a frying pan on medium heat, melt butter and oil. When foamy and bubbly, add patties and fry evenly about 5 minutes per side, until nicely browned.

{
While oil or water is added to tuna in the canning process, the liquid in canned salmon comes from the fish itself.
}

Left: Potted Herring (p. 73);
Right: Pecan Salmon Roll

PECAN SALMON ROLL

This is my variation of a recipe that I picked up on my travels in Lunenburg, Nova Scotia. I have used this versatile recipe on numerous occasions, both for myself and for events that I have catered. People never seem to tire of the tantalizing results from this simple preparation. Serve with a sliced baguette or crackers.

Makes 6–10 servings, as an appetizer

9 oz (250 g) cream cheese

2 tbsp goat cheese (optional)

1 tbsp lemon juice

1 green onion, finely chopped

1 tbsp creamed horseradish

½ tsp cayenne pepper

1 15-oz (425-g) tin salmon, drained

½ cup (125 mL) finely chopped pecans

2 tbsp finely chopped parsley, plus a few
   sprigs for garnish

In a bowl, cream together cheeses, lemon juice, green onions, horseradish, and cayenne pepper. Add salmon and mix to combine well. Refrigerate for at least 2 hours.

Shape mixture into a roll about 8 x 3 in (20 x 8 cm). Combine pecans and parsley and sprinkle onto a clean, dry surface. Roll log through mixture to cover. Place on a platter and garnish with parsley sprigs.

 For an Italian spin on this recipe, replace green onions, horseradish, and cayenne with 2 tbsp pesto sauce and 1 tbsp finely chopped sun-dried tomatoes; replace parsley with basil.

SALMON COULIBIAC

Some recipes are treasures just because they consistently live up to their sophisticated names. Coulibiac, a hot fish pie, is an innovation of Russian cuisine with worldwide appeal. So, from St. Petersburg, Russia, to St. Petersburg, Florida, this delicious dish is almost as fun to pronounce as it is to eat. This recipe is dedicated to the memory of Frank Von Zuben.

Makes 6 servings

1 lb (500 g) package puff pastry

2 7.5-oz (213-g) tins salmon, drained

1 package Uncle Ben's Wild Rice, cooked
    according to directions

2 tbsp chopped parsley

2 tbsp chopped dill

3 green onions, finely chopped

zest of 1 lemon

sea salt and freshly ground black pepper,
    to taste

4 eggs, hard-boiled

1 egg, well beaten

Preheat oven to 425°F (220°C).

Roll out puff pastry into 2 triangles 6 x 10 in (15 x 25 cm). In a large bowl, combine salmon, wild rice, parsley, dill, green onions, lemon zest, and salt and pepper.

Place 1 pastry triangle on an oiled baking sheet. Spread ½ of rice-salmon mixture over pastry, leaving a ½ in (1-cm) border. Arrange hard-boiled eggs in center, end to end. Spread remainder of rice mixture in an even layer over eggs. Brush border of pastry with beaten egg. Cover with second pastry triangle and crimp edges to form a tight seal. Chill in refrigerator for 1 hour.

Cut 4 small slits in top. Brush top with beaten egg.

Bake for 10 minutes. Reduce heat to 375° (190°C) and bake for 30 minutes more, until golden brown.

SALMON *AND* HORSERADISH TEATIME SANDWICHES

To add a little more depth to this sandwich, I often grate some apple into the mixture. Our beautiful, wild, and complicated salmon also pairs well with orange and tomato or cucumber and dill.

Makes 12 teatime sandwiches

1 4.25-oz (120-g) tin of sockeye salmon

1 tbsp creamed horseradish

1 tbsp mayonnaise

sea salt and freshly ground black pepper,
    to taste

1 tbsp butter (for buttering bread)

6 thin slices good quality white bread
    (or mix it up with whole wheat bread)

1 bunch Italian flat leaf parsley, leaves
    plucked from stem

In a medium bowl, combine salmon, horseradish, and mayonnaise. Season to taste with salt and pepper. Butter 3 slices of bread. Divide salmon mixture between 3 buttered slices. Top generously with parsley, then cover with 3 unbuttered slices.

Trim crusts and cut each sandwich into 4 triangles. Eat soon after preparation; they don't keep for more than an hour or so.

Sardines

If there is any one fish that seems to be born to the tin, it's the sardine. In countries like Spain, Portugal, and Italy, fresh sardines have long been a marketplace staple. For the rest of the world, a sardine would seem naked without the familiar tin. Part of the fun of making a toasted sardine sandwich is turning back the key of the tin to reveal all the little sardines nestled comfortably in their bed.

The true European sardine is the young pilchard—a fish belonging to the herring family. The name "sardine" is, however, applied to many small fish packed with oil or sauce in distinctive flat cans. In North America, where sardine fishing and packing are big industry, small Atlantic herring are usually substituted for the pilchard.

The following recipes provide several delicious as well as nutritious reasons for sardines to leave their tin. Sardines are a terrific source of iron and are good for you in many other ways: 100 g (about eight fish) packed with skin and bones intact provide forty percent of the recommended daily allowance of calcium and 100 percent of the vitamin D that is necessary for its absorption.

SARDINE, RED ONION AND CAMBOZOLA SANDWICHES

While shopping at a local market, I bumped into Craig, a friend of mine. When I told him about this book, he shared this recipe, a favorite of both Craig and his father.

Makes 2 servings

2 tbsp mayonnaise

4 slices sourdough bread

2 ripe tomatoes, sliced

sea salt and freshly ground black pepper,
   to taste

1 3.75-oz (106-g) tin sardines in spring
   water, drained

2 slices red onion, cut into rings and soaked
   in 2 tsp balsamic vinegar

4 oz (125 g) Cambozola cheese, cut into
   chunks

2 butter lettuce leaves, washed and dried

Spread mayonnaise on slices of bread. Layer with tomatoes and season with salt and pepper, if desired.

Remove backbones of sardines, if desired. Divide sardines between two sandwiches, pressing each fish slightly to flatten. Top with drained onions, dot with chunks of cheese, and finish with lettuce leaves.

 Sardine heads were used by the people of ancient Peru to fertilize their nutrient-deficient cornfields.

THREE TIN TAPENADE

Your can opener works overtime on this one, but it's worth it. This flavorful Mediterranean appetizer is quick to prepare and has the added benefit of satisfying a small crowd. Served on your favorite crackers, it goes particularly well with a robust red wine.

Makes 6–8 servings as an appetizer

1 3.75 oz (106-g) tin sardines in water, drained

1 1.75-oz (50-g) tin anchovies, drained and soaked in ½ cup (125 mL) milk for 10–15 minutes

1 6-oz (170-g) tin tuna, drained

1 garlic clove, coarsely chopped

1 small shallot, coarsely chopped

1 cup chopped, pitted black olives

¼ cup (60 mL) coarsely chopped pimento

1 tsp grainy Dijon mustard

6 tbsp olive oil

2 tbsp dry sherry

2 tsp fresh rosemary, plus a sprig for garnish

In a food processor, blend all ingredients until coarsely combined, about 30 seconds.

Place in your favorite serving bowl and garnish with a sprig of rosemary.

The sardine is fished in great quantities off the islands of Sardinia, from which it takes its name.

CURRIED SARDINES ON TOAST

For this recipe, I prefer sardines packed in tomato sauce. Consequently, the concoction goes very well with tomato soup, be it your own homemade version or a quality tinned product. Sardines packed in tomato sauce are considerably lower in fat and richer in omega-3 fatty acids than sardines packed in oil. A much healthier choice!

Makes 1–2 servings

1 tbsp butter, for curry

1 1/2 tsp curry powder plus a few pinches for garnish

1 tbsp flour

1/4 cup (60 mL) dry white wine

1/2 cup (125 mL) cream

2 thin slices multi-grain bread, toasted

1 tbsp butter, for toast

1 3.75-oz (106-g) tin sardines, packed in tomato sauce

1 green onion, sliced (green part only)

sea salt and freshly ground black pepper, to taste

In a small saucepan on medium-high heat, melt butter. Stir in curry powder and flour. Combine and cook until foamy. Gradually add wine, stirring constantly. Cook until a smooth paste is formed. Add cream in a steady stream, stirring constantly to prevent lumps. Continue to cook on medium heat and allow to come to a boil. Reduce heat to low while you prepare remainder of recipe. Stir occasionally.

Place oven rack in highest position and preheat to broil.

Butter toasted bread with remaining butter. Top each slice with two sardines, crushing slightly. Remove backbone if desired. Spoon prepared curry sauce on top, and garnish each slice with green onions, a pinch of curry powder, and salt and pepper.

Place under broiler until sauce is bubbly, 2–3 minutes, to heat sardines through.

SARDINE AND POTATO PANCAKES WITH LEMON-CHIVE MAYONNAISE

You may not think of the humble sardine as exceptionally glamorous, but this recipe will change your way of thinking!

Makes about 18 small pancakes

1 3.75-oz (106-g) tin sardines packed in water, drained
1 Russet potato, peeled and cut in half
1 small yellow onion, diced
½ cup (125 mL) flour
1 tsp baking powder
¾ cup (175 mL) buttermilk
1 egg
2 tbsp vegetable oil
2 tbsp chopped fresh rosemary
freshly ground black pepper, to taste
1 tsp olive oil
1 tsp butter
Lemon-Chive Mayonnaise (see p. 58)

Chop sardines into small pieces and place in a medium bowl.

In a small saucepan on high heat, boil potato for 5 minutes. Remove from water, let dry for 5–10 minutes, then grate. Add grated potatoes and diced onions to sardines.

In another bowl, combine flour and baking powder. Whisk in buttermilk, egg, and vegetable oil. Add mixture to potato-sardine mixture, then stir in rosemary and pepper.

In a frying pan on medium heat, melt olive oil and butter together. When bubbly, use soup spoon to pour potato mixture into pan, making small pancakes. Cook for about 3 minutes, until small bubbles form on top. Flip pancakes over and cook for another 3 minutes, until golden brown. Serve with Lemon-Chive Mayonnaise.

SARDINE BRUSCHETTA

While spending a month in a little village in Burgundy, I quickly adopted the apéro ritual. An apéro is an invitation to spend the hour before dinner with friends, enjoying a restorative libation and a bite of something to stimulate your appetite (see p. 155). This is one of my favorite little bites to share with my friends and neighbors.

Makes 14 snacks

1 tsp olive oil

1 tsp butter

2 shallots, finely chopped

2 garlic cloves, minced

½ tsp curry powder

2 tbsp dried currants

1 medium tomato, finely diced

1 3.75-oz (106-g) tin sardines, drained

3 tbsp chopped parsley

sea salt and freshly ground pepper, to taste

1 demi baguette

Preheat oven to broil.

In a medium frying pan on medium-low heat, add oil and butter. When butter is melted, add shallots, garlic, and curry powder. Sauté for 1 minute, stirring constantly. Add dried currants and stir for 30 seconds. Add tomatoes and sauté for 2 minutes, stirring constantly. Add sardines and sauté for 1 minute, until warm. Remove pan from heat and add chopped parsley. Season with salt and pepper.

Slice baguette into about 14 thin slices. Place under broiler for 30 seconds, until toasty on one side. Spread sardine mixture on untoasted side.

ROAST SARDINES AND LEEKS VINAIGRETTE

Roasting brings out the unique flavor of the sardines, and pairing them with leeks adds a sophisticated touch. This vinaigrette goes especially well with mashed potatoes, which absorb all the wonderful juices.

Makes 1–2 servings as a small plate

2 leeks, sliced

1 tbsp unsalted butter

2 tbsp olive oil

freshly ground pepper, to taste

1 3.75-oz (106-g) tin sardines packed in
   mustard

1 tbsp balsamic vinegar

zest of 1 lemon

sea salt and freshly ground black pepper,
   to taste

Preheat oven to 400°F (200°C).

Slice white part of leeks into ¼-in (5-mm) slices. Place in a bowl of cold water and toss lightly to loosen any dirt.

In a small oven-proof frying pan on medium-high heat, melt butter and oil together. Remove leeks from water and shake lightly. Add leeks to pan, stir to coat, and sauté for about 3–5 minutes. Grind pepper mill 3 times over leeks. Place pan in oven and roast for 10 minutes.

Add whole sardines to pan and toss gently with leeks, being careful not to break up sardines. Roast for another 3 minutes to heat sardines through.

Remove from oven and sprinkle with balsamic vinegar and lemon zest. Season with salt and pepper.

TEMPURA TRIO: SARDINES, CARROTS AND PARSNIPS WITH SOY MAYONNAISE

My memory of the Tsukiji fish market in Tokyo is perhaps the most remarkable of my journey to Japan. All the foods, the ritual, the culture that I experienced—not to mention the amazing meal I enjoyed in Osaka at Ohnoya, the restaurant where renowned Vancouver sushi chef Hidekazu Tojo earned his chopsticks—were so spectacular, I recommend that all foodies make Japan their next culinary destination. Did I taste anything in Japan that resembled this recipe? No, but when I prepare this dish, it evokes fond memories of Japan.

Makes 1 serving (if you're hungry)
or 2 appetizers

1 10-oz (283-g) package tempura batter
1 tsp sea salt
vegetable oil (for frying)
1 tbsp mayonnaise
¼ tsp Japanese soy sauce
1 medium carrot, peeled and sliced into
   ¼ in (6-mm) rounds
½ large parsnip, larger half peeled and
   sliced into ¼-in (6-mm) rounds
1 4.25-oz (120-g) tin sardines, drained
5 shiso leaves, for (edible) garnish

Prepare 1 cup (250 mL) tempura batter according to package directions. Add salt and set aside. (This makes more than you need, but I like to have a goodly amount to swish my fish and veg about in.)

In a small saucepan, pour oil to a depth of about 3 in (8 cm). Heat to 335°F (170°C). Or, test by dropping a bit of batter in oil; if it sizzles and fries quickly, it is hot enough.

Meanwhile, in a small bowl, combine mayonnaise and soy sauce and set aside.

Swish carrots and parsnips in batter until well-coated. Place 2–3 at a time in hot oil and fry for 3 minutes. (Be careful when working with hot oil!) Remove and drain on paper towel. Swish sardines through batter and fry for about 2 minutes. Drain on paper towels.

Arrange carrots, parsnips, and sardines on a serving platter. Garnish with shiso and a dollop of mayonnaise mixture.

GOLDEN PAPPARDELLE WITH SARDINES, FENNEL AND SAFFRON

This recipe was given to me by my best friend in Brooklyn, Rozanne Gold. I have changed it only a little.

Makes 2 servings

1 14-oz (398-mL) can plum tomatoes in
   purée
1 large garlic clove, minced
1/8 tsp cayenne pepper
1/2 tsp ground fennel seeds
1/8 tsp ground saffron
4.24-oz (120-g) tin sardines in water,
   drained and chopped
1 tsp olive oil
1 tbsp ground turmeric
pinch ground saffron
4 oz (113-g) fresh pappardelle pasta
1/4 cup (60 mL) grated Parmesan cheese

{ *Tip:* Both pots—one containing boiling water and pasta, the other with sauce—should be ready at the same time. You don't want to cook the sardines, just warm them through. }

In a shallow saucepan on high heat, bring tomatoes, garlic, cayenne, fennel, and saffron to a boil. Reduce heat and simmer for 10 minutes, crushing tomatoes with a potato masher as sauce simmers and reduces a bit. Stir in chopped sardines and olive oil.

Meanwhile, in another medium pot on high heat, bring lightly salted water to a boil. Add turmeric and a pinch more saffron and simmer for 5 minutes. Add pappardelle and cook about 5 minutes, until tender.

Drain pasta, shake to remove excess water, and transfer to 2 serving bowls. Pour hot sauce over pasta, sprinkle with Parmesan cheese, and serve.

Shrimp

I tasted shrimp for the first time at the age of nine. My mother was a lobby hostess at Vancouver's Hotel Georgia and she treated me to shrimp cocktail at the Cavalier Grill. After all these years, it remains one of my most elegant dining experiences. I can still remember the dashing waiters and the white linen tablecloths.

The term "prawn" is often used arbitrarily to describe large shrimp. In fact, the prawn belongs to a specific subgroup of shrimp that are caught in fresh water. Most shrimp are caught in the wild, but within the last decade, a third of shrimp worldwide have been farm-raised. Wherever it is found, shrimp is every bit as nutritious as any other type of fish, but much higher in cholesterol than most—to be avoided by those on cholesterol-reduced diets.

Much as I like tinned shrimp, I cannot tell a lie. Shrimp in the tin is not comparable to fresh. But when you pair this product with some sumptuous selections from your pantry, a kind of magic happens. You can entertain with the kind of delightful meal that brings to mind a genuine touch of sophistication.

CURRIED SHRIMP TOAST

Once upon a time, I catered parties—mostly cocktail receptions—where this fried morsel was always popular. I just recently added the curry powder to the recipe, which I enjoy, but you can make this without it and it's still delicious. Note: I use coconut oil, but a light vegetable oil also works well.

Makes 15 hearty portions

1 8-oz (230-g) tin medium shrimp

1 shallot, peeled and chopped

½ in (1-cm) knob ginger, peeled and chopped

¼ tsp sea salt

½ tsp curry powder

freshly ground black pepper, to taste

1 large egg white

5 slices good quality white bread, crusts removed, each slice cut into 3 strips

¼ cup (60 mL) panko bread crumbs

coconut oil, for frying

In a food processor, blend shrimp, shallots, ginger, salt, curry powder, and black pepper, and process until finely chopped. With motor running, slowly add egg whites and process until well combined.

On strips of bread, spread mixture about ¼-in (6 mm) thick. Dip shrimp-coated side in panko crumbs. Cover with plastic wrap and refrigerate (or freeze) for 1 hour.

In a large cast-iron or stainless steel frying pan on medium-high, heat about 1 in (2.5 cm) coconut oil. When hot, fry toast on both sides for about 2–3 minutes, until golden brown. (Be careful when working with hot oil!) Drain on paper towels and serve warm. You can serve as is, or cut in half for a bite-sized morsel.

SHRIMP AND MUSHROOM TOAST

The addition of mushrooms and Dijon mustard to Curried Shrimp Toast (p.126) adds a layer of French sophistication. You can serve these as is, or cut in half for bite-sized morsels.

Makes about 15 hearty portions

1 8-oz (230-g) tin medium shrimp

1 shallot, peeled and chopped

3 medium white or brown mushrooms, quartered

1/8 tsp each sea salt and freshly ground black pepper

1 tsp curry powder

1 tsp Dijon mustard

1 large egg white

5 slices good quality white bread, crusts removed, each slice cut into 3 strips

1/4 cup (60 mL) panko bread crumbs

vegetable oil, for frying

In a food processor, blend shrimp, shallots, mushrooms, salt, pepper, curry powder, and mustard, and process until finely chopped. With motor running, slowly add egg white and process until combined well.

On bread strips, spread mixture about 1/4-in (6 mm) thick. Dip coated side in panko crumbs. Cover with plastic wrap and refrigerate (or freeze) for 1 hour.

In a large cast-iron or stainless steel frying pan on medium-high, heat about 1 in (2.5 cm) vegetable oil. When oil is hot, fry bread strips about 2–3 minutes on each side, until golden brown. Drain on paper towels and serve warm.

NUGGET POTATOES ᴡɪᴛʜ TARRAGON SHRIMP

This dish is simple, impressive, and especially memorable when the tarragon is fresh from the garden and the nugget potatoes are new.

Makes 2–3 servings

½ lb (250 g) nugget potatoes

1 tbsp butter

1 tbsp olive oil

2 tsp chopped garlic

1 tbsp chopped fresh tarragon

1 4-oz (113-g) tin shrimp

¼ cup (60 mL) white wine

1 green onion, chopped

In a medium saucepan fitted with a removable steamer on high heat, steam potatoes for about 10 minutes. Remove from heat and set aside.

In a medium saucepan on medium, heat butter and oil until bubbly. Add chopped garlic and tarragon and stir for 1 minute, but do not allow garlic to brown. Add shrimp and wine and heat through, 2–3 minutes.

Slice potatoes into thirds and cover with sautéed shrimp. Garnish with green onions.

  Who are you calling a shrimp? While some species of shrimp are so tiny that they are barely discernable to the human eye, others can reach quite large proportions, often weighing up to 4 lb (2 kg).

SHRIMP EGG ROLLS

I've created two versions of this recipe, both very tasty. The more exotic variation calls for pear with shiso leaves (also known as perilla), which you won't be able to find at every corner store. Most Asian markets stock shiso leaves, however, and the extra effort of hunting them down is worth it.

Makes 12 egg rolls

1 4-oz (113-g) tin baby shrimp

1 cup (250 mL) canned crushed pineapple, drained

¼ cup (60 mL) mayonnaise

3 tbsp chopped cilantro

2 cups (500 mL) bean sprouts

2 green onions, chopped

½ package 6-in (15-cm) square egg roll wrappers

1 egg, well beaten

vegetable oil, enough for frying

{ Substitute 1 pear, peeled, cut into finger-size pieces and 12 shiso leaves for the pineapple and cilantro. }

In a small bowl, combine shrimp, pineapple, mayonnaise, cilantro, bean sprouts, and green onions. Divide mixture into 12 portions.

Lay an egg roll wrapper on a clean work surface so that it looks like a diamond shape. Place one portion of mixture in center and fold point of wrapper closest to you over filling. Fold in sides. Brush top point with egg wash, then roll into a tight cylinder. Repeat this process for all 12 portions.

In a small pan or wok on medium, heat oil until a strip of egg roll wrapper sizzles when dropped into it and floats to the top immediately. Place 3–4 rolls at a time in the hot oil and fry for about 3–4 minutes a side, until golden brown on both sides.

SHRIMP AND SWEET POTATO CAKES

After closing my restaurant, millions of crab cakes later, it took a while before I could make another one. I developed this recipe to prove to myself that I could make a wonderful shrimp cake as well. I'm glad to say that's just what I did.

Makes 2 servings

1 4-oz (113-g) tin shrimp
¼ cup (60 mL) grated sweet potatoes
2 green onions, sliced
1 small grated parsnip
1 tbsp lemon juice
¼ cayenne pepper
1 egg, lightly beaten
¼ cup (60 mL) chopped tomatoes
1 tbsp chopped cilantro
2 tbsp cornmeal
2 tbsp grated Parmesan cheese
1 tbsp butter
1 tbsp vegetable oil

In a bowl, combine all ingredients except butter and oil. Form into patties and set aside.

In a frying pan on medium heat, melt butter and oil. When bubbly, place cakes in pan. Reduce heat to medium-low and cook about 2–3 minutes, until browned. Flip with spatula and cook another 2–3 minutes.

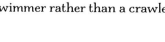

{ Unlike its close relatives, the lobster and the crab, the shrimp is primarily a swimmer rather than a crawler. }

ASIAN SHRIMP STIR-FRY

There are few things in a kitchen that are more fun to cook with than a wok. In less time than it takes to think about ordering take-out Chinese food, you could have finished this dish and felt so much the better for it. Serve over cooked rice or rice noodles. You may spice this dish up with a few sprinkles of chili pepper flakes.

Makes 2 servings

1 tbsp sesame oil

½ lb (250 g) oyster mushrooms

1 head bok choy, thinly sliced

3 green onions, sliced

¼ lb (124 g) snow peas

1 4-oz (113-g) tin shrimp

1 tbsp light soy sauce

In a wok over medium to high, heat oil. Add mushrooms and bok choy and sauté for 1 minute. Add green onions, snow peas, shrimp, and soy sauce, and sauté for 1-2 minutes.

{ The very first cans were oval in shape. These, however, proved to be unsuccessful and were soon replaced by the cylinder-shaped cans that we are familiar with today. }

SHRIMP *AND* SPINACH-STUFFED TOMATOES

Stuffed tomatoes may remind you of white gloves and garden parties, but this recipe deserves to be appreciated on a more regular basis. If you're in an elegant mood, you can stuff the mixture into cherry tomatoes. If you're having the "good ol' boys" over, use the beefsteak variety. Either way, this recipe makes a nice light luncheon when served with a salad.

Makes 2 servings

2 garlic cloves, chopped

½ red onion, finely chopped

1 tbsp olive oil

½ tsp dried chili flakes

1 4-oz (113-g) tin shrimp

1 lb (500 g) spinach, chopped and steamed

⅓ cup (75 mL) ricotta cheese

2 tbsp grated Parmesan cheese

freshly ground black pepper, to taste

2 medium tomatoes (or about 8 cherry tomatoes) sliced in half, flesh and seeds removed

Preheat oven to 350°F (180°C). Place rack in middle of oven.

In a frying pan on medium heat, sauté garlic and onions in oil with chili flakes for 1–2 minutes. Remove from heat and mix in shrimp, spinach, and ricotta and Parmesan cheese. Season with pepper, then stuff tomatoes.

Place tomatoes in a casserole dish and bake for 15–20 minutes, until nicely browned and bubbly.

PASTA RAMEKINS WITH SHRIMP AND GOAT CHEESE

I have made this dish without shrimp with great success for many years. Recently, I threw in some tinned shrimp on a whim, guessing that it would make the recipe even better. According to my party guests, my instincts were right. You can find pasta sheets in the fresh pasta section of most supermarkets. I like to serve this on a bed of wild greens that has been tossed with balsamic vinaigrette.

Makes 4 servings

2 fresh pasta sheets

3–4 tbsp melted butter

3–4 tbsp grated Parmesan cheese

5 oz (142 g) goat cheese

1 egg

1 tbsp heavy cream

3 sun-dried tomatoes, thinly sliced

3 fresh basil leaves, chopped

1 4-oz (113-g) tin shrimp

Preheat oven to 350°F (180°C).

Using a 3-in (8-cm) ramekin dish, trace 4 circles on pasta sheets (2 per sheet) with open (larger) end of dish and 4 circles with closed end.

Coat 4 ramekin dishes with about 1 tsp melted butter and Parmesan cheese. Place one of the larger pasta circles in each dish and fit snugly.

In a bowl, mix goat cheese, egg, and cream to combine well. Add tomatoes, basil, and shrimp and mix well.

Place mixture into lined ramekins. Top each with smaller pasta circle, brush with remainder of melted butter, and sprinkle with remainder of Parmesan cheese.

Bake for 15–20 minutes. Remove from oven, run knife gently around edge of ramekin, and turn out onto serving dish.

SHRIMP AND DILL QUICHE

The combination of shrimp and dill is truly a classic taste. What makes this recipe a little different is the addition of feta cheese. For an additional dash of Greek flair, try adding sliced Kalamata olives.

Makes 4 servings

1 9-in (23-cm) pastry shell
1 4-oz (113-g) tin shrimp
1 cup (250 mL) crumbled feta cheese
1/4 cup (60 mL) chopped green onions
2 tbsp chopped fresh dill or 2 tsp dried
2 large eggs
1 cup (250 mL) light cream
freshly ground black pepper, to taste
1/4 cup (60 mL) grated Parmesan cheese

Preheat oven to 375°F (190°C).

Bake pastry shell for 10 minutes. Remove shell from oven and lower heat to 350°F (180°C).

Distribute shrimp evenly over pastry, then cover with feta cheese, green onions, and dill.

In a bowl, whisk together eggs, cream, and pepper. Pour over shrimp mixture and sprinkle with Parmesan cheese.

Bake for 40 minutes. Let sit for a few minutes before slicing and serving.

Approximately 6 million (metric) tons of shrimp are produced worldwide each year.

TOASTED SHRIMP SANDWICH WITH CARROTS AND HAZELNUTS

I've adapted this recipe from an old cookbook put together back in the 1950s, by the women's auxiliary group of my mother's church. It's a nice change from a tuna sandwich, and provides the same sense of comfort.

Makes 2 servings

1 4-oz (113-g) tin shrimp

1 medium carrot, grated

1/4 cup (60 mL) chopped hazelnuts

2 tbsp mayonnaise

1 tsp lemon juice

cayenne pepper, to taste

4 slices toasted multi-grain bread

1 cup (250 mL) iceberg lettuce

In a bowl, combine shrimp, carrots, and hazelnuts. Add mayonnaise, lemon juice, and cayenne pepper and blend well but gently.

Lay out toast slices. Divide lettuce between 2 slices, top with shrimp mixture, cover with other slice, and cut in half.

Tuna

Growing up, most of us recall tuna as the main ingredient in two classic recipes: the tuna sandwich and the tuna casserole. To this day, the only drawback with the tuna casserole is that you can't wrap it in paper and take it to school. That's where the tuna sandwich comes in. As a child, it was my favorite brown bag lunch, and I practiced mixing together the right combination of tuna, celery, and green onion until I achieved the perfect balance. Other kids would attempt to trade their chicken sandwiches for it, sometimes offering to throw in a cookie or an apple. Of course, I always refused.

Remember those ads that referred to tinned tuna as Chicken of the Sea? Well, I always thought that was an insult to the unique flavor of tuna. After all, tuna has a noble history. Preserving the fish, drying it in small cubes, or pickling it in brine goes back to 525 BCE, and early recipes used seasonings such as cinnamon, coriander, vinegar, and honey. Canning tuna started in the late 1800s, providing a taste and convenience that has satisfied millions around the world. If you're still wondering why anyone would go to all the trouble to preserve tuna, then you've never been to my place for a tuna melt.

You may have gathered by now that I'm a bit of a tuna snob. I stick to the albacore (white meat) species for all my recipes. I don't mean to put down all the other varieties of tinned tuna, but I find the chunk form brings out all the best qualities that the fish has to offer. When purchasing tinned tuna, you should also consider what it's packed in. I buy tuna packed in water since this maintains the true flavor of the fish better than oil or brine. Besides, the oil tends to draw away up to a third of the nutrients from the fish as well as boosting the number of fat-based calories.

The great thing about tuna is that its true flavor will always come through in any number of recipes. What does tuna marry well with? Just about everything. In the following selection of recipes, I include tuna with pasta, potatoes, rice, and all varieties of vegetables, herbs, and spices. And so, with this selection, I happily liberate tuna in the tin from the comforting confines of the brown bag and the casserole. Enjoy.

TUNA  ARTICHOKE SALAD

In 1983, I visited New York City for the specific purpose of discovering unique food products. There I spotted my first bottle of balsamic vinegar, which I smuggled home in my suitcase. Of course, now most pantries include this delightful product. The use of balsamic vinegar in this recipe adds an Italian flourish. And to think I used to believe that the only reason to visit Modena (the birthplace of balsamic vinegar) was to stalk Pavarotti! Serve this with a hearty multi-grain bread for a nice lunch.

Makes 2–3 servings

2 tsp balsamic vinegar

2 tbsp mayonnaise

1 tsp lemon juice

1 6-oz (170-g) tin tuna, packed in water, drained

1 14-oz (398-mL) tin artichoke hearts, drained and quartered

2 green onions, sliced

2 tbsp pitted, sliced black olives

3 fresh basil leaves, chopped

freshly ground black pepper, to taste

2 butter lettuce leaves or 2 chopped romaine lettuce leaves

In a medium bowl, combine balsamic vinegar, mayonnaise, and lemon juice.

Add all other ingredients except lettuce and toss gently. Add freshly ground pepper to taste.

Arrange mixture on bed of lettuce leaves and serve.

Tuna—the largest member of the mackerel family—was caught and consumed by the Phoenicians 3,000 years ago. Believing that its tail brought good luck, they hung up the posterior part of the fish and devoured the rest.

New York Lunch

In my mind, New York City and tuna are the perfect match. I have fond memories of visiting Manhattan's Frick Collection, heading off to a deli for a tuna fix, and eating lunch on the steps of a brownstone. I remember feeling so very alive and happy at that moment. Was it the tuna or was it New York? This simple recipe, written down exactly as I remember it, proves that it very well could have been the tuna.

Makes 2 servings

3/4 cup (175 mL) small pasta shells, cooked according to package instructions

1 6-oz (170-g) tin tuna, drained

1/2 cup (125 mL) fresh peas, lightly steamed

1/3 cup (75 mL) diced red bell peppers

2–3 green onions, sliced

Dressing:

1 tbsp white wine vinegar

3 tbsp olive oil

sea salt and freshly ground black pepper, to taste

1/4 tsp each fresh tarragon, marjoram, and thyme or 1/8 tsp dried

1 tbsp chopped fresh parsley

Drain cooked pasta and rinse with cold water.

Place pasta, tuna, peas, peppers, and green onions in a bowl.

In a small jar, combine all dressing ingredients and shake well. Pour over tuna mixture and toss to combine well.

This recipe tastes best after 1–2 hours in the refrigerator.

{ Tuna packed in brine was once a crucial part of Mediterranean trade. So much so that the fish was featured on the coins of ancient Carthage and of Cadiz in Spain. }

APPLE, CHEDDAR *and* TUNA MELT

In high school, one of the first things I learned to make was the classic Tuna Melt. Proudly showing off my culinary achievement at home, I made several and promptly devoured them. It took a while before I could look at a Tuna Melt again, but this version rekindled my love affair.

Makes 2–3 servings

1 6-oz (170-g) tin tuna, drained

1 tbsp mayonnaise (or more, as desired)

1 tsp lemon juice

1/4 cup (60 mL) diced red onions

1/4 cup (60 mL) diced celery

1 Granny Smith apple, peeled and finely cubed

freshly ground black pepper, to taste

1 sourdough baguette

3/4 cup (175 mL) grated, aged Cheddar cheese

In a medium bowl, combine tuna with mayonnaise, lemon juice, onions, celery, and apples. Season with pepper and combine well.

Slice baguette into 8 pieces about 1/2-in (1-cm) thick. Cover slices with mixture, then sprinkle each with cheese.

Place rack in top portion of oven and turn on broiler. Place slices on a cookie sheet and put under broiler for 2–3 minutes, until warmed through and cheese is bubbly and begins to brown (don't let them burn).

In North America, only 5 of the 13 species of tuna are harvested commercially: albacore, yellowfin, bluefin, bigeye, and skipjack. Of these, only those tins with albacore are labelled "white meat tuna."

TUNA AND CANNELLINI BEANS IN PITA POCKETS

The pita pocket is a popular substitute for sliced bread. Snipping off the top and stuffing the pocket with an appetizing combination of ingredients is the ultimate in dining convenience. While the filling for this recipe is messy, the pita pocket provides the perfect solution.

Makes 2–3 servings

1 6-oz (170-g) tin tuna, drained

1/2 cup (125 mL) cooked or canned
   cannellini beans (drained if canned)

1/4 cup (60 mL) diced celery

1/4 cup (60 mL) chopped green onions

1/4 cup (60 mL) diced red bell peppers

6 mini pitas (about 4-in [10-cm] rounds)

Dressing:

1/2 tsp ground cumin

1 tbsp lemon juice

2 tbsp olive oil

freshly ground black pepper, to taste

In a bowl, combine tuna, beans, celery, green onions, and peppers.

In a separate small bowl or jar with a lid, add all dressing ingredients and whisk or shake to combine well.

Pour dressing over tuna mixture and toss. Snip off top of pitas and fill with mixture. Serve at once.

Apparently, the oval cans that were filled with fish for the Gold Rush miners of 1849 are the very "herring boxes without topses" worn as sandals by "My Darling Clementine."

Avocado, Tuna and Corn Relish Pita

This is tuna with a southwestern flair. Pairing tuna with avocado was such an easy thing to do. And, as with the Tuna and Cannellini Beans (p.144), the best way to eat this mixture is in a pita pocket.

Makes 2–3 servings

1 6-oz (170-g) tin tuna, drained

1 ripe avocado, peeled and cubed

1/3 cup (80 mL) kernel corn (fresh in
   season, or frozen)

1/4 cup (60 mL) diced tomatoes

1/4 cup (60 mL) finely chopped red onions

1/2 tsp seeded, chopped jalapeño peppers

1/4 cup (60 mL) diced red bell peppers

1 tbsp lime juice (or more, to taste)

1 tbsp olive oil (or more, to taste)

1 1/2 tsp minced fresh cilantro

sea salt and freshly ground black pepper,
   to taste

6 mini pitas (about 4-in [10-cm] rounds)

In a large bowl, combine all ingredients except pitas and mix gently to combine well. Fill pitas with mixture and serve at once.

{ In the United States, about 1 billion pounds of canned and pouched tuna are eaten per year. }

OUR PERFECT SALAD NIÇOISE

This recipe is from another book I wrote, Cooking for Me and Sometimes You. *I prefer to use quail eggs, but small chicken eggs can be substituted.*

Makes 2 servings

2 small eggs or 6 quail eggs
about ½ cup (125 mL) small green beans
   (haricots verts)
10 nugget potatoes
Anchovy Vinaigrette (see p. 19)
1 3.5-oz (100-g) tin albacore tuna packed in
   water, drained
10 cherry tomatoes, sliced in half
18 small Niçoise olives
2 tbsp chopped curly parsley
freshly ground black pepper, to taste

In a small pot on high, boil small eggs for 4 minutes or quail eggs for 2 minutes. Set aside to cool, then peel and cut into quarters. When using quail eggs, I peel 1 quail egg and slice it in half and keep the other egg unpeeled to decorate the salad, allowing my guests to peel their own.

In a medium pot on high, cook beans for 1 minute in boiling, lightly salted water. Remove from water and run under cold water for a few seconds.

In another pot on high, cook potatoes in boiling, lightly salted water for 10 minutes. Drain and let cool, then cut into quarters.

In each of 2 shallow bowls, place 1 tbsp vinaigrette. Add potatoes, beans, tuna, tomatoes, olives, and eggs, finishing with chopped parsley. Add another tsp (or, to taste) vinaigrette to each bowl and gently mix. Season with freshly ground black pepper and serve.

SESAME, GREEN BEAN *and* TUNA SALAD

This salad is designed as a light summer meal with a loaf of good bread. But it also is a welcome addition to any buffet featuring an array of interesting salads.

Makes 3–4 servings

Dressing:

2 tbsp Japanese soy sauce

1 tbsp sesame oil

2 tbsp sherry

3 tbsp olive oil

1 tsp brown sugar

½ tsp minced fresh ginger

sea salt and freshly ground black pepper,
    to taste

Salad:

1 lb (500 g) green beans, trimmed and
    sliced on the diagonal into 3 pieces each

1 small red bell pepper, sliced into strips

1 6-oz (170-g) tin tuna, drained

1 tbsp sesame seeds (roasted or raw)

1–2 green onions, sliced

In a small jar with a lid, combine all dressing ingredients and shake to combine well.

In a saucepan fitted with a steamer, steam green beans for just over 1 minute. Remove from heat and toss with dressing and red bell peppers.

Chill salad for about 1 hour (or more). Just before serving, toss with tuna and sprinkle with sesame seeds. Garnish with green onions.

{ Sorry, Charlie! For years, StarKist's principal advertising icon was Charlie, an erudite tuna. In his ceaseless efforts to be harvested by StarKist, Charlie tried to impress the company with his taste in poetry and classical music, but he always received the same response: "Sorry, Charlie. StarKist doesn't want tuna with good taste. StarKist wants tuna that tastes good." }

TUNA AND POTATO CASSEROLE

My mother made this recipe with yellow onions sliced in rings and a can of Campbell's Mushroom Soup. When I tried it for myself, I had to do it my own way. The use of heavy cream is not mandatory, but it does quicken the procedure. Regular or skim milk can be used if you want less fat. I even tried it once with soy milk.

Makes 2–3 servings

8 small potatoes, sliced ⅛-in (2-mm) thick

8 garlic cloves, peeled

10 pearl onions, peeled

freshly ground black pepper, to taste

1 tbsp olive oil

1 ½ tsp lemon juice

½ tsp chopped fresh rosemary or ¼ tsp dried

½ tsp chopped fresh thyme or ¼ tsp dried

½ tbsp butter

½ lb (250 g) sliced mushrooms

2 tbsp vegetable stock

1 cup (250 mL) heavy cream

1 6-oz (170-g) tin tuna, drained and flaked

½ cup grated Parmesan cheese

Preheat oven to 350°F (180°C), with rack in middle of oven.

In an 11-in (3-L) casserole dish, place potatoes, garlic, and onions. Toss with pepper, olive oil, lemon juice, rosemary, and thyme. Cover with lid or foil and bake for 20 minutes.

In a medium saucepan on medium-high heat, melt butter. Reduce heat to medium and add mushrooms. Sauté for 5 minutes. Add vegetable stock and half the cream. Let reduce for 2–3 minutes, then add other half. Reduce sauce to nice consistency: not too thick or too thin.

Remove potatoes from oven. Distribute flaked tuna in pieces over top of potato mixture. Cover with mushroom sauce and sprinkle with Parmesan cheese. Cover casserole and bake for 15 minutes, until potatoes are fork tender. Remove cover and bake for additional 3–5 minutes, until casserole is bubbling and browned.

TUNA ᴀɴᴅ RICE CASSEROLE

*To most people, tuna casserole means one of three things: with potatoes,
with pasta, or with rice. My mother made it with potatoes.
I find this rice version much more appealing.*

Makes 4 servings

2 tbsp butter
1 cup (250 mL) basmati rice
1/3 cup golden raisins
2 1/2 cups (625 mL) vegetable stock
2 6-oz (170-g) tins tuna, drained
2 tbsp butter
2 tsp curry powder
1/4 tsp ground ginger
1 cup (250 mL) sliced mushrooms
1/4 cup (60 mL) dry white wine
1/4 tsp dry mustard
1 1/3 cups (325 mL) heavy cream
2 green onions, sliced
3/4 cup (175 mL) grated Parmesan cheese
freshly ground black pepper, to taste

Preheat oven to 375°F (190°C).

In a medium saucepan on medium, heat 2
tbsp butter. Add rice and stir until well-
coated. Add raisins and vegetable stock.
Bring to a boil. Reduce heat to low, cover, and
simmer for 20 minutes.

Butter a 13-in (3.5-L) casserole dish. When
rice is cooked, spread over bottom of dish.
Distribute tuna evenly over top.

In a frying pan on medium-low heat, melt 2
tbsp butter. Stir in curry and ginger for 20
seconds, then add mushrooms. Sauté gently
for 3 minutes, then add wine. Sprinkle in dry
mustard, and stir until well-combined and
wine has slightly reduced. Slowly add cream
while stirring constantly, until mixture
reaches a medium to thick consistency.

Remove from heat, add green onions, and
spoon over tuna and rice. Top with grated
Parmesan cheese and season with pepper.
Bake for 20 minutes.

TUNA AND PASTA CASSEROLE

When my nephew, Dylan, was growing up, he didn't like potatoes or rice, so I created this dish for him. It could have any number of different ingredients added to it, but this is how Dylan likes it! It is particularly rich in calcium—great for combatting osteoporosis—because it contains both milk and cheese.

Makes 3–4 servings

1 tbsp butter

1 tbsp flour

1 cup (250 mL) milk

1 cup grated Cheddar cheese

4.4 oz (125 g) dried broad egg noodles

1 6-oz (170-g) tin tuna, drained and flaked

1/3 cup grated Parmesan cheese

freshly grated black pepper, to taste

Preheat oven to 375°F (190°C).

In a medium saucepan on medium heat, melt butter. Add flour and stir for about 1 minute. Slowly add milk and stir until sauce reaches a medium-thick consistency. Remove from heat, stir in grated Cheddar cheese, and stir until combined well.

Meanwhile, in another saucepan, cook noodles according to package directions.

Butter an 11-in (3-L) casserole dish and lay cooked noodles in dish. Cover with tuna, then pour cheese sauce over top. Sprinkle with Parmesan cheese. Season with pepper and bake for 10 minutes, until warmed through and bubbly and browned.

Today, most people make sure that their tin of tuna has a dolphin-safe symbol somewhere on the label. In 1990, North American tuna canners responded to one of history's most widespread consumer boycotts by announcing that they would no longer buy tuna that had been caught using drift nets, a fishing method that led to the drowning of millions of dolphins.

YAM, RED PEPPER and TUNA CASSEROLE

This casserole follows the same directions as the Tuna & Potato Casserole (p.149) but with different ingredients. Just another twist! Yams make it special; they are a good source of beta-carotene and vitamins A and B.

Makes 2–3 servings

1 large yam, peeled and sliced into ¼-in
(6-mm) rounds
½ medium red onion, sliced into rings
½ medium red bell pepper, chopped
1 tbsp chopped fresh basil or 1 tsp dried
freshly ground black pepper, to taste
1½ tsp olive oil
1½ tsp balsamic vinegar
1½ tsp lemon juice
1 tbsp butter
1 tbsp flour
1 cup (250 mL) milk
½ cup (125 mL) grated Parmesan cheese
1 6-oz (170-g) tin tuna, drained

Preheat oven to 350°F (180°C).

Place yam, onions, and peppers in an 11-in (3L) casserole and sprinkle with basil and pepper.

In a small bowl, blend oil, vinegar, and lemon juice, then toss with vegetables in casserole. Cover with lid or aluminum foil and bake for 15–20 minutes.

Meanwhile, in a saucepan on medium heat, melt butter. Mix in flour with wooden spoon and stir for 30 seconds—do not brown. Add milk slowly, stirring constantly. When mixture has reached a medium-thick consistency, add Parmesan cheese. Stir until well-blended, about 30 seconds, then remove from heat.

{
Aloha, tuna! In Hawaii, where a great deal of tuna is caught, albacore is known as *tombo*, yellowfin as *ahi*, and skipjack as *aku*.
}

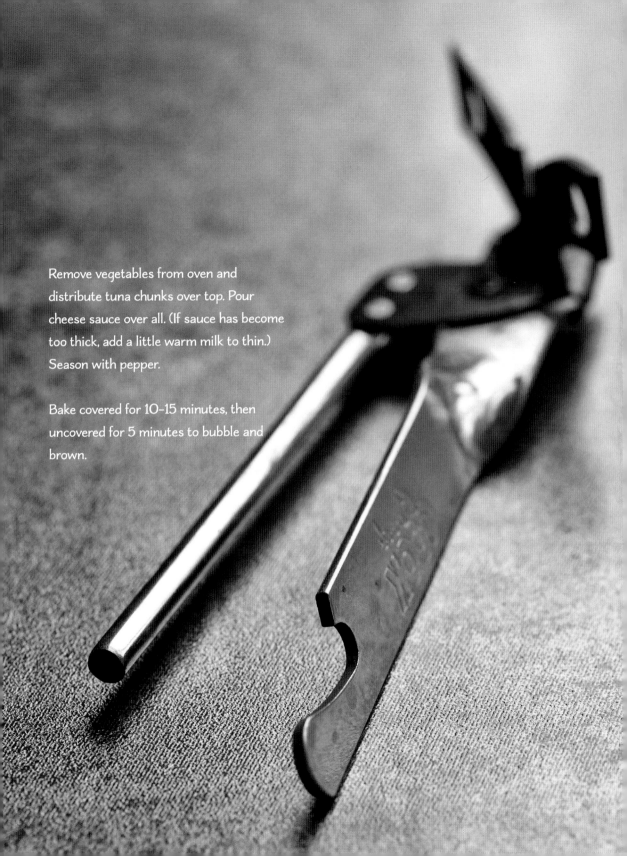

Remove vegetables from oven and distribute tuna chunks over top. Pour cheese sauce over all. (If sauce has become too thick, add a little warm milk to thin.) Season with pepper.

Bake covered for 10–15 minutes, then uncovered for 5 minutes to bubble and brown.

TUNA AND TARRAGON TEATIME SANDWICHES

When I took my French culinary training, tarragon was the herb; it was used in almost everything. For years, I rebelled against it. Now that I've spent more time in France, I have fallen in love with tarragon again. Arugula, chervil, basil, chives, and mint also pair beautifully with tuna.

Makes 12 teatime sandwiches

1 3.5-oz (100-g) tin solid white tuna,
  drained

1 tbsp finely diced celery

2 tbsp mayonnaise

zest of 1/2 lemon

1/4 tsp lemon juice

3 tbsp chopped fresh tarragon

sea salt and freshly ground black pepper,
  to taste

1 tbsp butter, for buttering bread

6 thin slices good quality white bread

In a medium bowl, mix tuna with remainder of ingredients, except butter and bread. Butter 3 slices of bread. Divide mixture between slices of buttered bread and cover with other slices.

Trim crusts and cut each sandwich into 4 triangles. Eat soon after preparation; they don't keep for more than an hour or so.

MENUS FOR A TINNED FISH TEA PARTY AND APÉRO

Rituals are the things that ground us, and I believe a day should not pass without at least one ritual involving restorative drinks.

Not every day, but on a good day, I will partake in both afternoon tea and apéro, one a British ritual, the other French. The first speaks to my British ancestry, which is, of course, with me every day, while France speaks to my heart, where I spend as much time as possible.

Afternoon tea occurs traditionally at four p.m., but I may decide at three that it is time for a cup of delicious black tea. A little bite of something, sweet or savory, is a must to balance the mood. This ritual encourages you to carry on for the rest of the day, whether you continue to do another hour or two of work or make a transition into the next phase of the afternoon. Many people entertain afternoon tea quests with sherry, sandwiches, and sweets. Here is a menu for a savory Tin Fish Tea Party:

Savory Anchovy Éclairs (p. 21)

Tuna & Tarragon Teatime Sandwiches (p. 154)

Salmon & Horseradish Teatime Sandwiches (p. 108)

Crab & Watercress Teatime Sandwiches (p. 61)

Spring Radishes with Anchovies & Crème Fraîche (p. 29)

Apéro is meant to be the hour (and just one hour) between the end of your work day and the evening meal. You can do this on your own or with friends; it simply involves the idea that you take an hour to restore yourself with a libation, allowing you time to decompress from the rat race, settle your mind, and prepare your belly for a relaxing meal and evening. You may pair a gin martini, or a glass of Lillet, sherry, or champagne, with any of the following:

Fried Anchovy Olives (p. 25)

Sardine & Potato Pancakes with Lemon-Chive Mayonnaise (p. 116)

Artichoke Dip with Tempura Anchovies (p. 23)

Sardine Bruschetta (p. 117)

Curried Shrimp Toast (p. 126)

Shiitake Mushrooms Stuffed with Crabmeat (p. 54)

INDEX